What Is a Book?

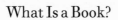

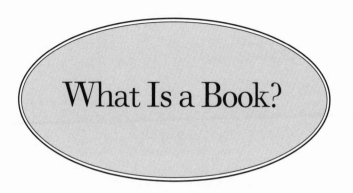

What Is a Book?

DAVID KIRBY

THE UNIVERSITY OF GEORGIA PRESS
Athens and London

Published by the University of Georgia Press

Athens, Georgia 30602

© 2002 by David Kirby

All rights reserved

Designed by Sandra Strother Hudson

Set in Monotype Walbaum by Bookcomp, Inc.

Printed and bound by Thomson-Shore, Inc.

The paper in this book meets the guidelines for
permanence and durability of the Committee on
Production Guidelines for Book Longevity of the
Council on Library Resources.

Printed in the United States of America

06   05   04   03   02   C   5   4   3   2   1

Library of Congress Cataloging-in-Publication Data

Kirby, David, 1944–

What is a book? / David Kirby.

p.   cm.

Includes bibliographical references (p.) and index.

ISBN 0-8203-2441-8 (alk. paper)

ISBN 0-8203-2478-7 (pbk. : alk. paper)

1. American literature—History and criticism.

2. American literature—History and criticism—Theory, etc.

3. Books and reading—United States.   4. Book reviewing—
United States.   5. Criticism—United States.   I. Title.

PS121 .K57 2002

809—dc21 2002002105

British Library Cataloging-in-Publication Data available

FOR JERRY STERN

1938–1996

Contents

Preface

While these essays were written recently over an eight-year period, they appear here as I approach my thirtieth year as a professional reader, that is, one who gets paid not only to read but also to talk and write about books.

Two very different circumstances form the backdrop to this selection, revision, and sequencing of a handful of critical essays from the one hundred–plus I published during that time. The first and most obvious is that the profession of English is now eye-poppingly different from what it was when I first entered it. How did this happen? How did the English department, the core of the classic liberal-arts campus, that bastion of calm and contemplation, that "city on the hill" that embodies the best of Western culture, become the hotbed of intrigue and internecine warfare that it is today? Much has been written on that subject, though I have seen nothing written by anyone who, by sheer happenstance, found himself, like me, in the No Man's Land between the two warring camps at the precise outbreak of the hostilities, as described in "What Is a Critic?"

The second stimulus for this book is less historical and more personal, and it originates in a time of pain for me and many others. In 1993 my friend and colleague Jerry Stern became ill with the cancer that would kill him. Jerry had begun work on an encyclopedia article on the developments in American literature for that year, but the chemotherapy and radiation left him too weak to go on, so he asked me to step in. His deadline for the article had already come and gone, but he had good notes, so I was able to finish the project, albeit hastily, to the editor's satisfaction.

Jerry continued the struggle against cancer over the next three years, finally succumbing to it in 1996. During this time he gave up all of his professional duties except his beloved teaching, holding classes at his house. With his encouragement and his editor's agreement, I took over the writing of the annual roundup on American literature for the encyclopedia. It wasn't as easy a task as it might sound: I had to condense a consideration of 150 or so titles into an essay of around three thousand words. Worse, I had to organize my remarks around a single theme: the decline of the family, say. But given the variety of the books I was considering as well as the fact that I had to cover not only novels, stories, and poetry but also criticism, biography, and history, how was this possible? My writing got more and more reductive as I folded and dog-eared writers' complex arguments so that I could fit them into my thematic pigeonhole. What should have been a dialogue became a monologue; the reductiveness that began to nag at me as I wrote the second annual article on American literature became intolerable to me as I wrote the third, so I was relieved when my application for a sabbatical in Paris was approved and I had an excuse to turn the job over to somebody else.

As different as these two circumstances were—the evolution of English from a gentlemanly profession to a paramilitary one, the writing of an annual article that began as a favor to a friend and ended in aversion—they shared a single characteristic, namely, a loss of love. There is only one reason to teach and to write about reading, and that's because you love books. Either you love books or you don't, and if you love them, you should treat them with respect, and if you don't, you shouldn't be teaching and writing about them (especially since you're probably not reading them). In his introduction to Sartre's *Nausea*, Hayden Carruth says literary critics are "a cheerless, canny breed, inclined always to say that a given work

has its good and bad points." Love for books comes first, though—
who approaches reading any other way?

What Is a Book? is organized around four principal essays, each
of which serves as the focal point of the book's four sections. The
first of these essays, "What Is a Reader?" deals with my experience
reading to children and how their love of certain kinds of books led
me to some assumptions on what adults love in books as well. The
second essay, "What Is a Writer?" discusses three characteristics
that all successful writers have. The third, "What Is a Critic?" is a
chronicle of the changes that have occurred, for better or worse—
and with some reservations, I think they have been mainly for the
better—in the profession of English during the past fifty years. The
final essay, "What Is a Book?" is based on a poll about favorite books
I took among various groups of readers, from high-school students
to university professors; it flows naturally out of the other three in
its assumption that well-informed personal preferences are more
important to book lovers than some critical hypothesis that was
true yesterday and laughable now. In the neighborhood of each of
these four central essays I have placed related pieces intended to
cast more light on the four terms under examination.

If there is an obvious difference in the sizes of the four sections, the reason for this difference is equally obvious. "What Is
a Reader?" and "What Is a Book?" are the shortest sections because I found reader and book the easiest of the four terms to define, whereas "What Is a Writer?" is a good bit longer than either
because the term "writer" is somewhat more problematic. And
"What Is a Critic?" is the longest section by far because "critic" is
the most contended term of all. Indeed, the very definition of the
word "critic" involves determining who is allowed to read books
and how they are allowed to read them and is thus at the heart of
the academic turf wars as surely as religion was at the heart of the
Crusades.

Another sort of natural imbalance lies in the fact that most of the examples I use in "What Is a Writer?" have to do with poetry because I am a poet myself: on the most personal level, I equate the words "writer" and "poet," so it seems natural to me to define the one in terms of the other. Conversely, most of the references in the essay "What Is a Book?" are to novels and novelists because, as I will explain there, it's a sad truth for us poets that most readers think of the words "book" and "novel" as all but synonymous. As the reader will see, I fight for my beloved craft literally to the last line of the last essay in this book, though both the reading public and the critical industry, as witnessed by the lopsided ratio of poetry to fiction reviews in the *New York Times Book Review*, seem destined to favor the prose narrative. (Brevity has its rewards, of course: poets may not write best-sellers or see their poems turned into movies, but John Barth remarked once that he didn't see his children grow up because he was too busy writing *Giles Goatboy*.)

There are certain ideas that run through the following essays that might best be summarized here so that readers who are engaged by them will know what to look for while those who find them repellent can take their own well-informed personal preferences elsewhere. They are these:

1. Devotion is more important than dissection. The first critical principle is the same as it was when you were in kindergarten: do you like the book or not?

2. Practice is more important than theory. Given the choice between sharing a train compartment with someone who has ten ideas and has read one hundred books or someone who has no ideas and has read a thousand books, I'd say take the latter.

3. Literary criticism will never dominate mainstream literary practices but will instead function as an absolutely essential element of them. As Montaigne said, raisins may be the best part of a cake, but raisins are not as good as a cake. Or, if you prefer sports metaphors, consider the one used by John Fowles to describe how criticism affects his novel-writing: it's like the bunkers on the golf

course, and while you take them into account, you don't play golf solely on the basis of where the bunkers are.

4. Good critical writing should also be good writing. Often literary critics make the language ugly by changing nouns to verbs as they "privilege" and "foreground" various objects and ideas (though creative writers, traditionally the guardians of language, are not guiltless in this matter, since they "critique" each other's poems and stories and even "workshop" them).

5. Like all good writing, good critical writing should say what it says as succinctly as possible. Tenure requirements call for massive tomes, but I rarely read a critical book that shouldn't have been an article, an article that shouldn't have been a note, a note that shouldn't have been a paragraph, a paragraph that shouldn't have been an epigram.

6. Everything being equal, the critical writings of the writer-critic will always be worth more than those of the person who produces criticism alone. The raisins-cake analogy applies once again: I find the theory of Slavoj Zizek and Julia Kristeva interesting, even breathtaking at times, but Henry James and Toni Morrison have more to say to me about other novelists' novels.

These are not necessarily ideas that Jerry Stern would have agreed with, but he would have discussed them with vigor, humor, and hundreds of examples to support or confute my arguments, which is why I have dedicated this book to him.

Acknowledgments

The four essays that provide the titles to the sections of *What Is a Book?* appeared originally as journal articles, sometimes in altered form and in an order of composition that differs from their sequence of appearance in this book.

"What Is a Critic?" is the earliest essay and appeared as "The New Candide, or What I Learned in the Theory Wars" in the *Virginia Quarterly Review* 69 (summer 1993), 393–407 (permission granted by the *VQR* to reprint this and the other *VQR* essays mentioned below). In this new version I have moved one large section to the essay entitled "Slouching toward Baltimore," where it seemed more at home; dropped two paragraphs near the end that no longer seem credible to me; and added more (and juicier) tales of academic infighting than appeared in the original.

"What Is a Writer?" was written second and appeared, largely in the form in which it appears here, in the *Virginia Quarterly Review* 72 (winter 1996), 75–85.

"What Is a Reader?" was written next and appeared originally as "The Secret Lives of Books" in the *Missouri Review* 20 (1997), 194–203. In this version I restore what I consider a key paragraph on Bruno Bettelheim that was cut from the original at the insistence of an editor who was disturbed by recent revelations about Bettelheim's unpleasant personal nature that, to me, took nothing away from the pertinence of his ideas.

It was at this point that I realized what I had thought were free-standing journal articles were, in fact, chapters of a potential book—light-flashes in my interior sky that were trying to become a constellation, in effect. With this in mind, I not only began to revise the other three essays but also wrote "What Is a Book?" and gave it the title I intended for the whole collection. Here it too appears largely as it did originally in the *Virginia Quarterly Review* 75 (spring 1999), 292–304.

In the time-honored academic way, then, I had, in effect, backed into my project: a consideration of the four basic elements of one of the most fundamental human transactions, namely, the making and consuming of literature. These core essays examine terms every kindergartner is familiar with: "reader," "writer," "book" as well as the slightly more specialized "critic." Having come this far, I began to seek topics that would cluster around my core essays and bring the ideas in them into better relief. These additional essays appeared first in these publications in England, Canada, and the United States: " 'The Thing You Can't Explain' " in *Ariel* (sponsored by the Board of Directors, University of Calgary), "The Poet as Pitchman" in the *Atlanta Journal-Constitution*, "Breakfast with the Cumaean Sibyl, or A Poet's Education" in *Parnassus: Poetry in Review*, "Is There a Southern Poetry" in *Southern Review*, "Mr. Post-Everything" in *The Virginia Quarterly Review*, and "M. L. Rosenthal and Our Life in Poetry" in the *Washington Times*.

The editors of two encyclopedias also commissioned articles that are used in my book in forms that differ occasionally from their original versions. "Emerson, Poe, and American Criticism in the Nineteenth Century" and "Ghosts and Gadabouts" appeared originally under the entries "American Literary Criticism since 1914" and "The Novel" in *The Continuum Encyclopedia of American Literature*, edited by Steven Serafin (New York: Continuum, 1999). Versions of "Slouching toward Baltimore," "Reviewers in the Popular Press and Their Impact on the Novel," "Born in the Marketplace," and "It Isn't about America, It *Is* America" originally appeared under the entries "Critics and Criticism: 20th Century,"

"Reviews, the Popular Press," "United States III (1850–1900)," and "The Adventures of Huckleberry Finn" in *Encyclopedia of the Novel*, edited by Paul E. Schellinger (Chicago and London: Fitzroy Dearborn, 1998). When the essays in *What Is a Book?* draw from works by other critics, those works are cited briefly in parentheses and then identified fully in the bibliography that concludes this volume.

Individually, these seventeen essays, which were chosen from the more than one hundred written during the same period, appeared in different countries; in journals that are sometimes readily accessible today and sometimes less so; and in no particular order. Here, they follow a discernible pattern and have been revised so that each relates to the whole.

The preface, like all prefaces, was written last. It echoes so many ideas that I have discussed in essays and reviews not included here and in classroom conversations and chats with friends and arguments with foes that it is, in many ways, the most thoroughly rehearsed of these essays, even though it appears for the first time here.

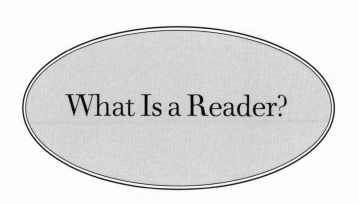

What Is a Reader?

What Is a Reader?

Every Wednesday afternoon during the summer I went to a local housing project to read to a group of children. With one or two exceptions, I never met the moms and dads. The children seemed to run the place: I'd park my car and start walking toward the rec room with my books, and someone, usually one of the Carter brothers, would shout, "Story Mannnn!" and the children would come running. I'd find a seat, the little ones would pile into my lap, the others would arrange themselves behind me, and we'd start.

I was never quite sure who would show up, so I always brought a variety of books with me, from the simplest picture books to ones that were longer yet could be finished in the hour we had together. Although they had definite preferences, the children were game for anything, whereas I preferred the longer books to the shorter. It goes without saying that there was never really any such thing as starting on time, so I would usually skim a couple of picture books until everyone had settled in and then start a longer story.

There was always a sort of rhythm to these sessions. The littlest children would pop their thumbs in their mouths and become progressively more glassy-eyed as the afternoon went by. None of them ever went to sleep, to my knowledge; instead, they were in a trance state analogous to the one I often find myself in while reading, even if I no longer suck my thumb. The children who were there to socialize, but who were too old or too rowdy to be read to, often gave up after a few minutes and either left voluntarily or, as happened more than once, were shown the door by me.

I enjoyed almost all my Wednesdays with the children, though I could have used a little more parental involvement: after the discipline problems, my major frustration was simply finding someone to open the rec room (or "the rec," as the children called it). In August, Tallahassee is unbearable unless its native climate is corrected by air conditioning on a gargantuan scale, and many times we had to sit outside under what shade we could find because the person with the key hadn't shown up and couldn't be found.

I always called it a good Wednesday, though, as long as Patrick didn't show. Patrick was a couple months shy of three, and since he wasn't really able to get much from an afternoon of quality literature, he was obviously there to be babysat. Unfortunately, Patrick developed a fierce attachment to me and insisted on sitting in the middle of my lap rather than on the bony outposts of thigh or knee to which he pushed his older but less aggressive rivals. Patrick did not have perfect control of his bodily functions, and more often than not, it seems, an acrid odor would fill the air fifteen or twenty minutes into the story. The other children, proud of their own self-discipline, would chide him: "Patrick, you have pooped in your pants!" Patrick would counter with the indignation that only a guilty party could summon, and I would have to squander valuable time restoring the peace.

Most of the children were good listeners, by which I mean they were active, calling attention to something that excited them or asking what a word meant. Two or three always brought snacks, which they shared freely, and on those days I sampled some of the grimiest candy I have ever eaten, not to mention various gums, pops, powders, and fried snacks flavored with agents not to be found in nature. Usually, some of the fourth-grade girls—the sisters Sophie and Danya, perhaps one or two others—moved around behind me at some point and began to silently braid my hair.

I read to the children every Wednesday because I had seen a notice in the paper calling for literacy volunteers. Mainly, though, I was there because I missed reading to my own children, who were now too old for it. I love children's books, but I have always found that reading them silently and alone is a little like reading a play instead of watching it or, more to the point, acting in it. At his insistence, I read to my older son Will until he was nearly fifteen, and when he sat in my lap, his legs stretching out beyond mine and his arms hanging nearly to the floor, it was like cradling a colt. (Not coincidentally, one of my favorite scenes in children's literature occurs in William Steig's *Sylvester and the Magic Pebble,* in which the young donkey Sylvester, freed from a magic spell and restored to his ecstatic parents, drapes himself across their laps with his legs sprawling.)

Will's younger brother, Ian, ended his nightly reading sessions earlier, when he was around twelve, but he participated in them more aggressively as long as they continued. Ian didn't like going to school at first. At that time, I was reading him fairy tales, though after a while it got to the point where he wanted to hear only the story of Thumbling. Thumbling, of course, is the child of a poor peasant who says to his wife, "How sad it is that we have no children! With us all is so quiet, and in other houses it is noisy and lively." His wife sighs and says, "Yes, if we had only one, even if it were only as big as a thumb, I should be quite satisfied, and we would still love it with all our hearts." Sure enough, she gives birth to a child, and, equally surely, he is born small and stays that way. But size is no obstacle to someone with as much pluck as Thumbling, and he has all sorts of adventures and even makes a lot of money for his parents, for, as the story tells us, Thumbling is "a wise and nimble creature, and everything he did turned out well."

Now not only did this become Ian's favorite story, but when I got to his favorite line, he'd say, "Read that again," and I'd say, "Thumbling was a wise and nimble creature, and everything he did turned out well," and Ian would suck his thumb and smile and look off dreamily. I could tell he was thinking of the many benefits of being wise and nimble and all the fun a wise and nimble person might have and all the rewards he'd get. And before long Ian decided that school wasn't such a bad place after all. It was a good venue for the practice of wisdom and nimbleness; it was a place where, with a little luck, things might even turn out well.

These were not necessarily conscious thoughts Ian had, and they are certainly never ones he expressed to me. His relation to "Thumbling" was simply a matter of asking for the story over and over and listening to it and taking what lessons from it he could and gradually finding that school wasn't such a bad place after all. Children almost never say why they like or dislike a particular book, partly, I suspect, because they don't have the vocabulary to articulate their deep reasons and partly because, in many cases, they would be embarrassed to say why.

In his marvelous book *The Uses of Enchantment*, Bruno Bettelheim builds much of his defense of traditional fairy tales around a statement a character makes in Djuna Barnes's novel *Nightwood*: "Children know something they can't tell; they like Red Riding Hood and the wolf in bed!" In fact, as the cover illustration of his book, Bettelheim chose Gustave Doré's provocative illustration of Red Riding Hood gazing at her bed partner, a decidedly nasty-looking wolf, with a mixture of horror and fascination. Bettelheim's book is controversial because many of the traditional tales he defends are not politically correct. But the fundamental advice he gives parents is undeniably sound, as I learned from my experience with Ian: read story after story to your child and let the child pick his or her favorite. It will be the right choice, even if the child can't or won't say why.

The children I read to on those summer afternoons also had their favorites. It is something of a commonplace to note that children prefer the classics to contemporary stories, and I saw some evidence to that effect. *Snow White* and *Cinderella* were favorites among the girls, who had not heard about feminism yet and were still looking forward to the arrival of the handsome prince. The boys were not especially interested in handsomeness; the Carter brothers asked for *Beauty and the Beast* repeatedly and would echo the Beast in deep Transylvanian voices when he asked Beauty, "Do you think I am very ugly?"

All my Wednesday children were beautiful in the sense that their faces were open, radiant, unclouded. The Carter brothers were beyond that; with their soft, lustrous skin and big-toothed smiles, they were positively seraphic. But as they thought about that beast and how ugly he was and how he both despised his ugliness and, at the same time, reveled in it, they crossed their eyes and let their tongues loll out of their mouths and tried to be as repulsive as possible.

In general, though, I noticed that the children liked stories that involved secrets. Maurice Sendak's *Where the Wild Things Are* and *In the Night Kitchen*, *Peter Pan:* these tales of transformation and revolt against adult norms were to my children as Halloween is to a regular school day. Their absolute favorite and the one book I was asked to bring back with me every time was Malcolm Bird's *The School in Murky Wood*, in which a group of monster children and their monster teacher break into a school every night and act sloppy and stupid and mess up the place and then clean it just before dawn so that the regular students and teachers don't notice anything amiss.

It drove the children mad with joy to think that monsters might have been in their classrooms at Barnes Elementary the night before and had slouched in their desks and scrawled gibberish on the board and dumped pencil shavings on the floor but then left without a trace, so that no one knew they had been there except the monsters and, now, the children themselves. There was a secret bond between the imaginary monsters and the real children, and neither side would tell.

Conversely, a book they didn't like was one called *Willie's Not the*

Hugging Kind, which is the story of a tough little guy who learns that it's okay to show your feelings after all. It was not a book I cared for, but it was one of the few I could find with African American characters in it, and I didn't think it right to restrict my audience to a 100 percent Snow White diet. As it turned out, my Wednesday children were more color-blind than I was, so in the end Willie and his feel-good family lost out to princesses and fairies and monsters. The latter, for what it's worth, tended to be either various combinations of yellows, greens, and purples or else so completely covered with hair that you couldn't tell what color their skin was.

And so I would read to the children, and the older ones would read to me, and the little ones would get glassy-eyed, and Patrick would fill his pants, and Sophie and Danya would braid my hair. The children always wanted me to stay longer than the one hour, but I found those hours pretty intense, especially on the days when the rec was locked up and we had to read outside in the Tallahassee humidity.

When it was over, I'd drive home and let myself in and go up the stairs to my wife's study. Our schedules are chronically out of sync, so Barbara and I are always startling each other with our unexpected appearances. As I come through her door, she turns from her computer screen and sniffs the air suspiciously and then her mouth falls opens in surprise. There I am before her, looking, in all respects except one, like a standard middle-aged *fin de siècle* English professor with my Gap shirt and pants, sneakers, and scuffed leather briefcase, my graying blond hair twisted into tight dreadlocks.

What kinds of books do adults like and why? Freud knew the answer to both questions: adults like murder mysteries, and they like them because murder mysteries answer the child's primal question, namely, what is going on behind Mommy and Daddy's door? Daddy is growling, Mommy is moaning. Is he hurting her or is it something else? Is it sex or death or both? Any way you look at it, it's a secret.

It may be no accident that the record best-seller of recent times is a novel that is built around a secret. Robert James Waller's *The Bridges of Madison County* enjoyed a 162-week stay on the *New York Times* best-seller list for all sorts of reasons, not the least of which is the torrid affair between the frustrated farm wife and her most excellent lover. But it occurs to me that a significant part of the story's appeal is that the Francesca character not only sacrificed her own happiness by staying with her family but also kept the affair secret until after her death, which is when her children find out what happened behind that particular door.

What an appealing story: you have the great sex and the swell emotions that go with it, yet you do the right thing by your family, so you get to feel noble, mainly, though you also get to feel guilty for screwing the handsome stranger as well as sorry for yourself that you didn't run off with him. And it all takes place in secret, which means no venting, no messy catharsis: the feelings redouble on each other, becoming thicker and tastier as the years go by.

I knew a woman once who said that, as a child, whenever she wanted to feel joy and disgust at the same time, she waited until her mother left the kitchen and got the tube of anchovy paste out of the refrigerator and squirted a big gray glob of the salty stuff on her tongue and swallowed it down, shuddering with the ecstasy of knowing she'd done something stupid. Once her mother came back unexpectedly and asked her why she had that expression on her face, and my friend gave the universal kid's answer of um-UM-um and ran from the room. Because if she explained it wouldn't be fun any more; it wouldn't be nasty.

Now *The Scarlet Letter* is a book similar in many ways to *The Bridges of Madison County*. It's got a frisky heroine, a fairly decent if not downright foxy lover, and a dull, off-screen husband, and here too the affair is secret. A difference between the two books is that Waller's, like a murder mystery, contains only one secret, whereas Hawthorne's contains many. Waller serves up an affair and conceals it; Hawthorne does the same while managing to engage religion, history, the judicial system, medicine, even astronomy and optics—did that meteor that passed over in chapter 12 really spell out a big "A" in the sky or did it just look as though it did?

In great books, there are always many elements that defy explanation. That is why there will be half a dozen new books and a hundred articles on Hawthorne this year; there will always be more questions than there are answers. To put it another way, great books contain, not many secrets, but too many secrets.

To go back to Freud's door for a moment: I have referred to secrecy in mysteries, popular fiction, and canonical literature, but pornography is based on secrecy as well. Yet in the order of things, pornography is generally considered inferior to these other types of writing not so much because it is immoral, I think, but because it is narrow, since it only has the one subject. It's no accident that one of the classic porn films is entitled *Behind the Green Door*. When you open that door, you get Marilyn Chambers. But that's all you get.

I didn't really have to read to all the children at the housing project, of course, since the older ones could read the books I brought as well as I could. But there is a difference between reading and being read to, and even the older children liked to hear someone else's voice. We speak often of the mind's eye. But there is also a mind's ear, something we are most acutely aware of when we read poetry, with its strategic emphases. Children don't have that mind's ear yet because they haven't had that much experience at listening.

But they want to have it, so they listen. When my own boys were younger and the family took trips together, they would fall asleep before we left the driveway; it was as though the car's rear doors emitted a narcotic gas as soon as they were closed, an odorless, invisible vapor that never made it as far as the front seat. Barbara and I stayed alert and chatty, catching up on topics we'd put aside during the packing, reminiscing over past trips or planning future ones, recommending or denouncing books or movies or people we knew.

From time to time, I would become aware of movement just over my shoulder. I'd glance back, and there would be a small head, the hair looking as though a bird had just flown out of it, the cheek brightened by a line of drool, the eyes starting from their sockets, glazed yet searching. You'd think it was Roderick Usher or another of Poe's neurasthenics, but it was only one of the boys, leaning forward to listen to us talk. We could be talking about anything—adjustable-rate mortgages, say—and that child would hang in there for miles, just to hear the words. Sooner or later the sleep gas would get to him again and he'd fall back, joining his insensible brother, whose own head would appear before long, also thirsty for the rhythms of speech. That gas was powerful, but I could see them fighting it, because the spoken word is powerful, too. Children love secrets, but they also love conversation, which is secrecy's opposite.

My Wednesday children and I didn't spend the whole time reading; far from it. Sometimes we used the books as springboards for conversation, and sometimes we just talked. They weren't the best-behaved group of individuals I've ever met, and occasionally I became too disgusted with them to read at all, so we would just sit there until the ruckus of the moment had consumed itself, and we'd talk.

Once Jarrod Carter was driving me crazy, so to give him something to do, I asked him for his autograph. I ain't got no autograph, he said. Sure, you do, I said, and let him write his name on the back of my hand: see, that's your autograph. Somebody shouted, "I want to autograph you, Story Man!" and then everybody wanted to. But I didn't want those children to be sticking their pens into me; to eat their grimy candy was enough of a health hazard. So I produced the only piece of paper I had, a subscription card for

Foreign Affairs Quarterly that I had picked up off the library floor earlier that day and was using as a bookmark. Jarrod signed it first, filling in the blank for the subscriber's name.

I still have that card. You should drop that thing in the mail, Barbara says; Jarrod would be the only first-grader at Barnes Elementary with his own subscription to *Foreign Affairs Quarterly.* But I like to look at their signatures: Jarrod T. Carter, Jamaal L. Carter, Mary L. Sanchez, Jessica C. Davis. How proud they all were of their middle initials! Remember when you were that age? The Ts and Cs and Ls were the alluring I've-got-a-secret center of our very beings; they were enticements to conversation that no one could pass up. "What's the T for?" "Thomas." you'd say, or "Tatiana." "I ain't saying," you'd say, but that would just lead to more cajoling, more guesswork, more talk.

My favorite conversationalist was a girl named Yolanda. She had ideas on everything, and she loved to complain, especially about the boys and how much they got away with in Mrs. Hightower's class at Barnes Elementary. They say they want to go to the beach, she says, but they pronounce it like the dog. And they ask to use the dictionary, but they say the first syllable real loud.

Thinking that we should probably be talking about something else, I ask Yolanda what she wants to be when she grows up. "I don't know," she says, "but I know one thing. I don't want to have a whole bunch of these children," and she waves her hand dismissively at everyone else.

By this time Sophie and Danya have had enough of Yolanda and all the attention she's getting, so they tell me Yolanda's real name isn't Yolanda; it's Sheniqua. "Your name's Sheniqua?" I say to Yolanda. "Why did you change your name from Sheniqua? That's a beautiful name." "Oh," she says and waves her hand again, "it's a bunch of Sheniquas out there."

When our time is up, some of the children insist on helping me pack and leave. Jarrod usually carries the books for me, and Jamaal takes the keys out of my pocket so he can unlock the car door. I have long since learned to leave my spare change at home, not because of the minimal financial loss but because of the altercation that ensued the one time Jamaal came up with some nickels that the others pounced on.

I'd like to be able to say the children were being good scouts, but the real reason they wanted to help me was so that they had an excuse to search my car. They would go over that sucker like narcotics agents, digging up stuff I didn't even know I had. Once somebody came up with a pocket-size German dictionary I hadn't seen for years. "This ain't English!" somebody else shouted. "It's German," I said. "Want to learn German? The first thing you need to know is, 'Sprechen sie Deutsch?' "

"Sprechen sie Deutsch!" they shouted. And then they all ran off to beat the crap out of the kids who didn't know what the words meant yet. "Sprechen sie Deutsch!" they'd shout as they punched their little friends. "Know what that means? Huh? Do ya?"

When the fall term began that year, the Wednesday sessions stopped. For one thing, my university duties began to require more of my time. But even if my job hadn't taken me away, I don't see how I could have continued to read to the children because I never could get someone to open the rec on a regular basis. I asked if I could be given a copy of the key, but somehow that couldn't be done, either. It was hard enough to read outside during the sweltering August afternoons. With the days getting shorter and the cold coming, it would have been impossible. The adult world stymied me, and, unlike Thumbling, I wasn't wise enough or nimble enough to stymie it.

I have said something about the reading preferences of adults and how they, like children, are drawn to books about secrets. Now I spend all my time with the in-between generation, the eighteen- to twenty-two-year-olds who have put children's literature behind them and are just beginning to make their own adult book-buying decisions. So what do they like?

I'm not sure I know. I'm not sure they know, at least not with the certainty of, say, Yolanda/Sheniqua on the one hand or my wife, Barbara, on the other. With a few exceptions, my students are so busy that they don't have the time for pure pleasure reading that the younger and older readers seem to have. They have full course loads; they have jobs, often full-time; a surprising number, married or not, have children. Others have been driven mad by the numerous social opportunities a university environment offers. And then there are the classic time-killers that plague everyone's existence: failed love, sexual betrayal, dysfunctional houses and cars, the death of relatives. Or, as one of my students said to me after several absences that came suspiciously close to Mardi Gras, "My grandparents were killed in a wreck again. . . ."

My students read a tremendous amount, of course, but they read what I and my colleagues tell them to read. How much fun can that be? I try to make it as much fun as possible: the Board of Regents of the State of Florida requires me to assign papers, give grades, and so on, but I try to remind my students as often as I can that the fundamental test of a book is still the kindergartner's test: do I like it? And when the papers have been assigned and written and collected and graded and returned, the book will still be there and still be likable, though its likability may have to do more with the secrets it retains rather than the knowledge it divulges. The German theorist Wolfgang Iser said that all great texts have a "fundamental asymmetry," by which he means the writer deliberately leaves gaps for the reader to fill.

So the books aren't born symmetrical, but they become that way, and it is the reader who makes them so, because whether or not it has monsters in it, every great book is a monster. Perhaps not surprisingly, many great books do contain monsters: *The Odyssey,* Ovid's *Metamorphoses,* the Old Testament, *Beowulf,* Dante's *Inferno, Gargantua* and *Pantagruel, Don Quixote, Gulliver's Travels, Frankenstein, Moby-Dick,* and *The Hunchback of Notre Dame,* not to mention the tall tales of Paul Bunyan and other American folk heroes as well as their counterparts in other cultures.

"Fine, fine," say my students. "Very informative, Doc. But we still have to write our papers. Got any tips?" "Yes, I do," I tell them. "My advice to you, John T. or Jane Y. Student, is to listen to the book. You've read it, so now listen to what it has to say: what it really has to say, not what someone else, even I, says it says. And listen to everything it has to say, not just part. Then all you have to do is fill in the gaps as best you can.

"And if that's not enough, you might try listening to what the books have to say to each other." In his brilliant mock slave narrative *The Oxherding Tale* Charles Johnson points out that a true slave narrative like Frederick Douglass's has its roots in St. Augustine's *Confessions* as well as the Puritan autobiographical tradition represented by writers like William Bradford. So that's four books talking to each other right there.

Imagine yourself in the library after hours, I tell my students. You went to sleep and woke up to find yourself locked in. You were able to find the snack machine in the dark, and you had enough change to get some cheese crackers and a Mountain Dew. You read for awhile by the streetlight that came in through the window, but your eyes began to hurt, so you stopped. It's after midnight, but only just. You've got a lot of hours ahead of you, and you're bored. You sit there and think how dumb you are, and then you hear it: a faint crackling sound, like insects or children in the distance. It's the books, telling their secrets to each other. Suddenly, you're not dumb any more. You're incredibly lucky, as it turns out, because all you have to do is sit there and listen.

Now there's a catch, of course, but isn't there always? Or, as Jarrod and Jamaal and Yolanda would say, "Sprechen sie Deutsch?" Because even though we can hear the books talking, we know that we won't be able to hear everything they say.

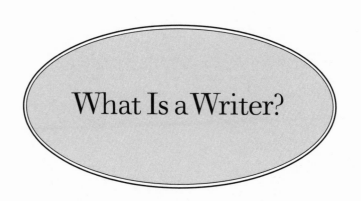

What Is a Writer?

What Is a Writer?

At this time in our culture, there are two extreme views of writers. The most conservative view sees writers as genuine heroes, gifted geniuses who are more insightful than the rest of us and who are therefore obliged to lead and instruct. The most radical view sees writers as history's lucky ducks, figures who, possibly because so many of them were white and male, were in the right place at the right time—that is, in a place of privilege—and who therefore often represent nothing more than a culture's most antidemocratic values.

Neither of these views is satisfactory, because each assumes the writer's passivity. According to the first, the writer was born special and, by writing a little now and then, sprinkles specialness on those of us who were not so lucky. According to the second, which assumes even more authorial passivity, the writer had specialness thrust upon him by the powerful and like-minded in his society and therefore, like an Aeolian harp, expresses the most oppressive of that society's values.

I would like to think that I know a little bit about writing, in part because I have written professionally for more than three decades but mainly because I have studied other writers for roughly the same period of time. And I have studied them in the way that yields the best results for the student, which is to say that not only have I read but I have also written about them.

Not that I always knew what I was doing, either as a writer or as a student of writing. I am both a poet and a critic, which means that I

only encourage distrust in both camps, with my critic friends wondering why I would wallow in something so messy and subjective as
poetry and my poet friends wondering how I could possibly squander the precious time I might use for versifying on the crafting of
footnotes. And, as I say, I have asked myself these same questions.
Not so much about the poetry, which I have written ever since I
could write at all and which seems as natural to me as walking or
breathing, but mainly about the criticism, which, after all, calls for
trips to the library, the reading of page upon page of soporific prose,
and other strenuous, unaesthetic activities.

Nonetheless, even as I turned out poem after poem, I also wrote
article after article and book after book of my own about other writers. "Why are you doing that?" the poets asked. And I had to say to
them, "I don't know." Because I knew I was looking for something,
but I did not know what.

Now I think I know. Now I understand that, on a less-than-
wholly-conscious level, I was looking for some kind of equation,
a formula to explain what a writer is. Recently I completed a book
on Herman Melville, and with the writing of that book came an
almost-complete understanding of what a writer is and what he or
she does. The Melville book became the keystone in the arch I was
constructing, although I still had a little work to do on the entire
structure before I was finished.

In many ways, Melville was the archetypal writer: neither the
genius nor the mouthpiece that some people think an author is
but one who was lucky and unlucky, stable and unstable, blessed
and cursed. Primarily, Melville was eccentric in both the figurative and the literal meanings of that word. That is, he was a little odd psychologically—more than a little, perhaps—but he also
spent much of his life on the margin of everything that might be
considered conventional.

If you are familiar with the rudiments of Melville's life, then you
know that there is a sound biographical basis for the unmistakable

presence in Melville's work of both a fondness for and a suspicion of rootlessness—and, one may as well say, a fondness for and a suspicion of permanence, too. Descended from prosperity, Melville was compelled by circumstances to exchange the stability of home and family for a life among some of humanity's most desperate characters: mutineers, deserters, common criminals. The suffering he saw and experienced as a young sailor repelled him, yet it was his maritime adventures that gave him his first—and, in his lifetime, his only—literary success. Even after he had published widely, married, and, by starting his own family, meticulously reclaimed his bourgeois birthright, Melville seemed often to feel the constraints of conventional life, and twice in later life he made sea voyages that mimicked the days of his penniless yet carefree youth.

It is no wonder that Melville's work is shot through with ambivalence and outright contradiction. But this does not mean that his career defies description; to the contrary, Melville's career poses a singular challenge that I tried to meet in my book on him. In attempting to view Melville as individual, citizen, and artist, I tried to write neither the biography of an author nor a critical study of the works produced throughout his career; instead, my goal was to write a biography of that career. The footnotes that I spent so much time on were intended to guide the reader toward the many worthwhile books and essays on Melville's personal history and on his writings and away from the inferior ones, but the text itself focuses on the life of his most intense self, that is, his writer-self: how it developed, how it functioned, how it reacted to success and failure.

The Melville book is the fourth and, unless circumstances convince me otherwise, the last in a series of books I have written, books that, though very different in subject manner, nonetheless are of quite similar construction. They deal with Reconstruction writer Grace King, with novelist Henry James, and with contemporary poet Mark Strand. Like the book on Melville, each of the others is also the biography of a career. A career as a writer is highly inadvisable; like actors and musicians, most writers don't succeed, and the ones who do still have to cope as much with failure as with success—and even success can be problematic, as the headlines tell us.

What I have learned from my four subjects, though, and from Melville most definitively—so definitively that, as I say, I see no need to write another book of this sort—is that successful writers have two traits in common, no matter how different they may be otherwise. The first is that they never give up. The second trait, one closely related to the first, is that they adapt.

Grace King, for example, is best known for her short stories, though she also wrote full-length fiction, literary criticism, and history. James wrote fiction of every possible length but also biography, criticism, plays, reviews, travel essays, and art criticism. Strand is one of America's preeminent poets yet is also the author of short fiction, children's books, and essays; in addition he has edited anthologies and translated the works of other poets.

What we see in each of these cases is dogged persistence matched with a consummate versatility. Here I am reminded of the story of what the physiologist Claude Bernard is supposed to have said to a student who asked how he might succeed in Bernard's laboratory. *Travailler comme une bête*, said the scientist: work like an animal, that is, with the persistence of an animal and an animal's disregard for failure, because, deprived of its bone or nut, an animal will not dwell on the absence of the thing lost but look elsewhere for another, without resentment.

In some instances, these writers moved deliberately from one genre to another, though in others they had no choice. James, for instance, was literally hounded from the theater after the failure of his play *Guy Domville* and wrote movingly in his notebook on January 23, 1895: "I take up my old pen again—the pen of all my old unforgettable efforts and sacred struggles. To myself—today—I need say no more. Large and full and high the future still opens.

It is now indeed that I may do the work of my life. And I will."
And he did: in less than a decade he published what many consider
his three greatest novels, *The Wings of the Dove*, *The Ambassadors*,
and *The Golden Bowl*, works built largely around scene, dialogue,
and other dramatic conventions he mastered during his "failed"
foray into the theater. (Incidentally, late in life James tried again
to write plays, with little more success than before.)

But even more than these other writers, Melville demonstrated
throughout his career an aggressive resistance to discouragement;
when he found one door closed to him, he looked around until he
found another that was open. His only truly popular books were essentially travelogues, and his great uneven masterpiece *Moby-Dick*
was largely ignored by a world that was not ready for it. Yet during
the decades of public silence that followed the realization that his
fictions were no longer marketable, he wrote the poems that alone
would have guaranteed him a permanent if minor position in U.S.
literature. And as he lay on his death bed he was writing "Billy
Budd," one of the finest short fictions of his or of any time.

But to say that Melville's life was a triumph because he wrote
a masterpiece as he lay dying is to overlook the genuine struggles
that punctuated his daily existence. It is easy to look back and say,
"Poe was a genius" or "Emily Dickinson wrote some of the finest
lyric poetry ever" and not recognize the many vicissitudes that
characterize the lives of everyone and perhaps the lives of artists
especially. We need to look more deeply: if persistence and adaptability are all, then the life of every writer would be a steady ascent,
with success a certainty.

Yet one of the paradoxes of understanding any celebrity, writer
or not, is that the better known someone becomes, the harder he
or she is to know. Even family members may be left in the dark;
Eleanor Melville Metcalf, Melville's own granddaughter, wrote in
her memoir that "the core of the man remains incommunicable:
suggestion of his quality is all that is possible."

The problem is compounded when the figure under scrutiny lived in the last century, a time when records were scarcer, photographs cruder, and descriptions couched in an English often foreign to contemporary ears. With a figure as inscrutable as Melville, the problem of understanding becomes almost insurmountable. He had achieved fame with his early, fact-based writings; startled the literary world with *Moby-Dick;* and then followed that masterpiece with the highly idiosyncratic *Pierre,* a book so strange that one newspaper ran the headline "HERMAN MELVILLE CRAZY."

In the end, of course, he produced a body of work that permanently altered the consciousness of a culture. For one thing, through his own eccentricity and that of his characters, Melville predicted better than any writer of his time the ambiguities of the twentieth century, thereby paving the way for such writers as William Faulkner. In *William Faulkner and Southern History,* Joel Williamson notes that Faulkner's greatest books, such as *The Sound and the Fury* and *Light in August,* were about people who had lost their grasp of their racial or sexual identity. The novelist himself had a nature as protean as Melville's and, like Melville, he was as capable of a crippling inconsistency as he was of a range and depth that gave his work immense power. Williamson notes that Faulkner took every conceivable position on civil rights for African Americans, from unstinting support to callous dismissal.

Here I am reminded of what William Pritchard says in his essay on T. S. Eliot in *The Columbia History of American Poetry,* that "it may even be the case that a great writer's power is commensurate with his power to offend," for inconsistency of character is double-edged. On the one hand, a protean nature puts the writer in touch with so great a variety of feelings and ideas that it can only be viewed as useful; on the other, it leads to the kinds of mistakes that constant, steady people are unlikely to make.

This inconsistency is, of course, perfectly normal. That is, inconsistency is perfectly human: while each of us would like to begin in the lower-left corner of the chart of success and rise on a straight line to the upper-right corner, the fact is that—and this is only if we are lucky—the careers of most of us, regardless of what field we have chosen, are marked by peaks and valleys and thus describe, not a straight line like the one an arrow makes as it flies toward the bull's-eye, but a jagged one that better resembles the little graph of the Dow-Jones Industrial Average, a psycho-economic ideogram that reminds us that while "Buy low, sell high" is sound advice, we cannot triple our capital through desire alone.

Readers should not expect writers to do what they themselves cannot, that is, get better every time. But it happens, and, like Melville before him, Faulkner became a victim of his own success when his readership found that his late works weren't as "well written" as his early ones.

Yet the curious thing about Faulkner is that, as Williamson notes, "none of his books had ever been met by a flood of rave reviews and an eager market." Instead, his celebrity status, his growing reputation in intellectual circles, and the awards and honors he had received (rather than the actual books he had written) turned him into a Great Writer. Thus, when a book like *A Fable* appeared late in life, the public didn't really know what to do with an author whose work they had never read in the first place.

But these kinds of vagaries are commonplace in the career of a writer and, indeed, are inseparable from the whole concept of writerly success. Another kind of turbulence is much more serious, however, and much more troubling to the writer than the mere ups and downs of the marketplace, and here I refer to the demons of mental and emotional illness. Again, we do not know as much about Melville's psychic makeup as we do about those of artists who lived after Freud rather than before. But there seems little doubt that Melville suffered from clinical depression; at several junctures his wife seemed ready to leave a husband grown insufferable, and there is no doubt that his little family breathed a collective sigh of relief when Melville disappeared for months on one of his voyages of renewal to Europe and the Holy Land. Faulkner's letters reveal him as anxious, irritable, and depressed, and his troubles with alcohol are well known. Yet both these writers worked steadily, met their obligations, raised families, made and kept lifelong friends— they functioned, that is, and led lives in many ways similar to yours or mine.

The fact remains, however, that many, many writers are so spectacularly disturbed that it almost seems axiomatic that the best writers are mad. Take, for example, Virginia Woolf, one of the finest novelists of the twentieth century as well as a manic-depressive and, eventually, a suicide. An editorial on madness and creativity in the *New York Times* notes, "An increasing number of psychiatrists, neurologists and geneticists . . . believe there's a link between the genius and madness of artists such as her. Maybe so. But as anyone who's ever read Woolf's letters and diaries can attest, it's the link between imagination and self-discipline that got her a place in literature's pantheon. Her mind may have had a grasshopper's fleetness, but her industry was the ant's" (October 15, 1993). Noting that Byron, Shelley, and Coleridge suffered from either manic depression or severe depression and that the composer Robert Schumann starved himself to death when he was forty-six, the *Times* piece quotes Dr. Ruth Richards as saying that "people who have experienced emotional extremes, who have been forced to confront a huge range of feelings and who have successfully coped with those adversities, could end up with a richer organization of memory, a richer palette to work with." Obviously, mental illness by itself has no direct relation to creative activity, or everyone with bipolar disorder would be an artist.

Besides, the idea that the only good writer is a crazy writer puts a tremendous burden on the writer who is talented, ambitious, and, perhaps to his or her disappointment, unredeemably sane. A poet friend of mine fretted about this in my presence once. "Maybe I'm too normal to be any good." I assured him he was a fine writer, and, in fact, he recently won a prestigious prize for his first collection of poetry.

Even so, I myself sometimes wonder if I am too happy to produce work of great feeling. The creativity of Melville, Faulkner, and Woolf cannot be explained by persistence and adaptability alone; great writers have these same traits, but so do great orthopedic surgeons and corporate presidents. Is mental and emotional illness the missing third ingredient in literary genius, and, if so, where does that leave the "healthy" writer?

In completing my formula, it is fortunate that I have my experience as a teacher of writing to fall back on. For, like all but a few writers I know, I make most of my living by doing something other than writing. And, like most of those in this situation, that means I teach.

Not all writers teach, of course. Melville was a schoolmaster for two brief periods in his life, and Faulkner did some celebrity stints as a professor late in life. But, for better or worse, neither had the thirty-year classroom career that is more or less standard for teacher/writers today. Artistically, no doubt this was to their advantage, since teaching is so time-consuming. However, in teaching writing one learns about it as well, and the lessons one learns that way can be invaluable.

In the writing classroom I have learned that, all things being equal, there are only two kinds of writers, namely, what I call the "unconscious" writer who produces very "conscious" material and then his or her antithesis. This first type of writer is the one who proclaims defiantly a contempt for tradition and who then, in total ignorance of what he or she is doing, unconsciously writes the most cliché, hackneyed work imaginable. The second type of writer is the one who consciously connects to the work of other writers through study and discipline, which is to say that this writer encounters a vast range of feelings and ideas, not through personal

experience, but through the experiences of others. You might say
that this second kind of writer is taking a correspondence course
from the School of Hard Knocks; the lessons may not be as vivid,
but the tuition is a whole lot cheaper. At any rate, it is this conscious writer who is more likely to produce work rich with deep
unconscious resonances, that is, the only kind of work that truly
satisfies.

In fact, this intellectual and emotional engagement with other
writing unites the healthy and the disturbed writer in a manner
far more important than any difference in emotional states could
possibly separate them. A writer is necessarily a fan of writing, and
fandom is an essential characteristic of every writer, whereas the
presence or absence of illness is an arbitrary factor having little in
itself to do with literary output. Even the briefest look at the life of
James or Woolf or Faulkner or any of the writers mentioned above
reveals that when they were not writing, most likely they were
reading and in that way banking the literary capital that makes
writing possible.

Still, it is for good reason that one connects mental and emotional
illness to artistic production. What illness does is provide the compulsion to write: to figure things out, as it were, to bridge a gap between oneself and others or to fill a hole that seems to exist in one's
life. As I write these words, Paul Mariani's *Lost Puritan: A Life of
Robert Lowell* has just appeared. The surface of the poet's life was
chaotic to the point of tragedy, yet Lowell's bouts with bipolar disorder achieve a kind of sameness after a while, and what lingers in
the reader's memory is a sense of the poet's monumental intellectual achievement. As regularly as he took himself off to one hospi-
tal or another, Lowell also went on periodic retreats to study, write,
translate, and, mainly, to read, read, read, from the earliest writers
up through the emerging poets of his day. It is evident that Lowell brought to these study sessions the kind of ferocity that often
disturbed his relations with wives, lovers, employers, and friends,

but it is also evident that from these sessions came the bricks with which the poet made his art.

For a less-troubled writer than Lowell, the compulsion to make one's life whole through study and organization and productiveness will be just as evident though much less frantic. However, the material that is studied and organized into what I have called the bricks of art will be the same. In a sense, it might be said that, though Lowell had a very rough time of it psychically, he had an easier time of it artistically than my poet friend who feared he was too normal. After all, Lowell *had* to read and write; for my friend, it is a matter of choice.

So in addition to what I have learned from studying writers, namely, that the best of them are (1) persistent and (2) adaptable, I have learned something else, both through my research and also through teaching writers, which is that good writers, be they healthy or ill, are (3) passionately devoted to literature. It is this third trait that makes the eminently successful person into a successful writer, just as, to use the examples I have already given, one might expect successful orthopedic surgeons and corporate presidents to be persistent and adaptable persons who are devoted, not to literature, but to their own fields of endeavor. Thus what sets successful writers apart from other successful types is the particularity of this third trait (i.e., literariness) and not illness, although it should be noted that the public is likely to be more tolerant of mentally and emotionally disturbed poets and novelists than it would be of similarly troubled doctors and business leaders. Let artists be grateful for this tolerance of the foibles of some among them, then; equally, let no one assume that you have to be crazy to write.

Assume, however, that one is quite persistent, adaptable, devoted to literature, and also at least intermittently sane; does this mean that one will be a great writer? Of course not, although it is doubtful one could become a great writer by any other means. At some point in the discussion of art, rational inquiry ceases, and observers from every discipline agree only on what cannot be said. Freud, for example, observes that "before the problem of the creative artist, psychoanalysis must, alas, lay down its analysis." An autobiographical James character (Dencombe, the novelist in "The Middle Years") says, "We work in the dark—we do what we can—we give what we have. . . . The rest is the madness of art." And Georges Braque, Picasso's contemporary, says, "In art there is only one thing that counts—the thing you can't explain." If all writing is an attempt to explain what cannot be explained, perhaps that is why there always have been and always will be writers. And if total explanation is foredoomed and partial explanation the only reasonable goal, the writers who succeed to the extent that they do will be the ones who are persistent, adaptable, and passionate enough to continue the search.

As I look back on my formula, with its two general traits common to all successful people and its one particular trait related to success in a particular area, I must admit to being somewhat dismayed at its simplicity. On the other hand, these simple conclusions are the result of long study of the four accomplished writers I have written books on as well as the dozens of others I have studied less formally and the hundreds of budding writers I have taught. Besides, regardless of how accurate the formula may or may not appear to the reader, I cannot think of any writer who would deny its implicit imperatives. For these are the things that, consciously or half-consciously, writers say to themselves each day: keep at it, be flexible, and, when not writing, read.

So at a time when some readers want to think of writers as gifted geniuses and others are bent on destroying the concept of authorship altogether, a close look suggests that successful writers are necessarily neither more brilliant nor luckier than other people but more persistent, more adaptable, and better-read, that is, more familiar—in a literary sense, at least—with the entire geography of the human mind and heart.

Breakfast with the Cumaean Sibyl,
or A Poet's Education

I am eating breakfast in the International House of Pancakes with my son Ian, the weightlifter, when we overhear the following conversation:

UNIDENTIFIED CUSTOMER: What's the difference between "Viva la French Toast" and "French Toast"?

IDA (A WAITRESS): The Viva come [*sic*] with an egg and two strips of bacon.

Ian and I look up at each other with big, stupid grins and then tuck into our meals, his a steak and eggs combo and mine a stack of pancakes, syrup and butter on the side.

Ian is a scholarship student, a good writer, but one far more taken with science than metaphors: he wants to be either a doctor or a dentist ("one of those guys in white coats"), though at the moment he's trying to get the right number of protein grams into himself so he can tear into one more monster workout sometime later today. I, on the other hand, who am pale, wheezy, and myopic from devoting most of my waking hours to literary work of one kind or another, am avoiding animal protein like the plague it is, at least to the sedentary.

As different as we are, though, each of us recognizes and revels in what we've just heard, which is poetry. It's poetry because it's heightened language instead of ordinary language, including the mispronounced "Viva" (which is, of course, "Vive" on the menu, as befits the imaginary country of origin of the dish) and the colloquial *s*-less "come."

But what we've just heard has two other qualities as well. It doesn't make sense, at least on the surface, just as no poetry makes sense the way, say, the words on the back of a box of cereal do. You could even argue that the conversation between Ida and the customer is ridiculous, at least as ridiculous as "That was a high year, fox-colored, like a crosscut redwood stump or vine leaves on the hills in November" (Czeslaw Milosz) or "Evening strains to be time's vast, womb-of-all, home-of-all, hearse-of-all night" (Gerard Manley Hopkins).

But in addition to being ridiculous, the overheard conversation is also vital: it's about breakfast, after all, food, calories plus pleasure. William Carlos Williams wasn't kidding when he wrote, "It is difficult / to get the news from poems / yet men die miserably every day / for lack / of what is found there."

Not everybody would agree that the conversation Ian and I overheard that morning is poetry, but then a lot of people would say Milosz is writing prose and Hopkins spinning cotton candy. The point is that poetic language is different from ordinary language, different to the point of strangeness, even, yet poetic language is absolutely essential to our mental and emotional well-being. How else are you going to get your Vitamin P?

Arguments about both the definition and the value of poetry go back at least to the Cumaean Sibyl, a crusty old gal who is supposed to have offered nine oracular books to King Tarquin the Proud in the sixth century B.C. When the king proved unwilling to meet her price, the Sibyl destroyed three of the books and offered the remaining six for the same amount, and when he balked again, destroyed three more and offered the remaining three for the original price. Being merely proud, not stupid, Tarquin bought the remaining three books, which were housed in the Temple of Jupiter on the

Capitol in Rome and consulted in times of crisis until the temple burned in 83 B.C.

That should have been it for the oracles, but the emperor Augustus had a new collection of utterances brought in from various corners of his empire. These Sibylline oracles were known to the Greek and Latin fathers of the early Christian church, who thought they contained valuable prophecies for the church, though later it was determined that the oracles were not uttered by the Cumaean Sibyl or any of her sister oracles but written by Jews and Christians imitating the original in such a way as to entice converts into their religions.

But as with the Shroud of Turin, who cares? It takes a special kind of idiot to go around saying, "It's not real, you know." Facts, shmacts: the Cumaean Sibyl lives on. You can see her likeness on the floor of the cathedral in Pisa, and she's also represented in the Sistine Chapel (by Michelangelo) and the church of Santa Maria della Pace in Rome (Raphael). In literature, the Cumaean Sibyl foretells the future to Virgil in the *Aeneid* and guides him through the underworld, and she shows up again in the epigraph to *The Waste Land* as a shriveled creature in a bottle who, having asked Apollo for long life, forgot to ask for youth and now asks only to die.

Yet even more important than the venerable political, religious, artistic, and literary heritage of the Cumaean Sibyl is her continued presence just over the shoulder of anyone reading poetry today. What Erato is to poets, the Cumaean Sibyl is to readers. As Charles O. Hartman notes, the sibyl would write the separate words of her prophecies on leaves and fling them from her cave, and it was up to her supplicants to gather the leaves, put them in the proper sequence, and interpret the results; they might get "toast" on one leaf, "viva" on another, and "French" on a third, but then they'd have to take it from there.

Conveniently, the second installment of Sibylline oracles, those collected by Augustus, were written in hexameter verse. So which is the real poetry, the free verse that has been lost or the extant (if ghost-written) hexameters? One way or another, say the four authors under consideration here, it's those hexameters. Even free verse (or "nonmetrical" or "unmetrical" verse, depending on who's doing the labeling) is written in a state of awareness of those absent meters, though what that state is and how aware the poet is and what meters are being mourned or scorned or subverted varies radically, as do opinions on almost every other point, from author to author.

The only one of these four books I can recommend without reservation—the clearest written, the most genial, the best informed—is Alfred Corn's *The Poem's Heartbeat.* Written out of a perceived need (Corn says in a preface that when he began to teach prosody he found only out-of-print, incomplete, or inaccurate textbooks), this handy guide starts with the assumption that the reader knows nothing of prosody or even such simple matters as what a line is:

> The word "line" comes from Latin *linea,* itself derived from the word for a thread of linen. We can look at lines of poetry as slender compositional units forming a weave like that of a textile. Indeed, the word "text" has the same origin as the word "textile." It isn't difficult to compare the compositional process to weaving, where the thread moves from left to right, reaches the margin of the text, then shuttles back again to begin the next unit. This motion, a slow progress from left to right, followed by a quick left reversal before beginning again, is part of both writing and reading, a kind of pendulum-swing intrinsic to the reading of poetry. Since the oscillation occurs more times per minute than the parallel experience of reading prose, it contributes to the hypnotic quality of poetry. What may or may not be obvious is that poetry has never fully disengaged itself from its associations with shamanism; the poet, like the shaman, has mastered certain techniques—rhythmic, performative, imagistic, metaphoric—that summon the unconscious part

of the mind, so that, in this dreamlike state between waking and sleeping, we may discover more about our thoughts and feelings than we would otherwise be able to do.

Typical of Corn's writing throughout, this passage moves easily from the simple (the line) to the complex (poetry's hypnotic potential) in a way that neither confuses the novice nor insults the veteran. Having inadvertently invoked the Cumaean Sibyl, who presents us with material designed to engage "the unconscious part of the mind," Corn begins a slow ascent through stress, meter, syllable, stanza, and every other purely mechanical aspect of poem-writing, which combine to produce what William Carlos Williams called a "machine made of words," a contraption that, properly assembled, is a mere clanging watchworks that can nonetheless leave the reader writhing with ecstasy like that of the supplicants gibbering before the mouth of the Sibyl's cave.

Concerning metrics, Corn notes how the peculiar qualities of English dictate our metrical system. Whereas there is a strong stress differential in English, there is none, for example, in French. Too, syllable length is less uniform in English (compare the monosyllables "smack" and "smooth") than in French, which is why French lends itself to syllabic verse, in which number of syllables per line signify rather than stress. So whereas German, which has an even stronger stress differential than English, bases its prosody on stress alone, the relatively younger English, which shares both French and Germanic elements, looks to both strong stress differentials and number of syllables per line as components of meter.

A second chapter deals with poetic feet, a subject Corn treats with typically casual hands-in-pockets scholarship. Actually, I go him one step better (or lower) by trying to lock the poetic feet into my students' crowded memories with homey, one-word examples:

iamb (iambic) unstressed-stressed, as in "balloon"
trochee (trochaic) stressed-unstressed, as in "gavel"

anapest (anapestic) unstressed-unstressed-stressed, as in "over-turn"

dactyl (dactylic) stressed-unstressed-unstressed, as in "avalanche"

spondee (spondaic), stressed-stressed, as in "railroad"

As with every aspect of metrics, a certain tolerance for others' examples proves necessary here, since these examples will be pronounced differently by different people, even from the same family: "po-LICE" is an iamb to old cosmopolitan me, but "PO-lice" is a trochee, in the Deep South manner, to my quondam farmgirl mom. Corn's contribution to the science of metrical variation comes at the end of his second chapter, where he discusses the general rule of substituted feet in a line not outnumbering the reigning meter ("in iambic pentameter you may make as many as two substitutions but not three—because then there would be more substitutes than iambs in the line").

A later chapter deals with "phonic echo": rhyme, yes, but also double rhyme ("seated" and "greeted"), triple rhyme ("verily" and "merrily"), half-double rhyme ("pure" and "during," "restrain" and "zany"), elided rhyme ("cresset" and "nest," "fervid" and "curved"), and so on. He argues persuasively that the ear does not like familiar rhymes ("wife" and "life"), monosyllabic or other same-syllable rhymes ("penniless" and "wretchedness"), or rhymes involving the same part of speech ("take" and "shake"). An excerpt from Hardy's "The Darkling Thrush" shows how a skillful rhymer not only practices but conceals his art:

> So little cause for carolings
> Of such ecstatic sound
> Was written on terrestrial things
> Afar or nigh around,
> That I could think there trembled through
> His happy good-night air

Some blessed Hope, whereof he knew
And I was unaware.

Of the four rhymes, only one is monosyllabic ("through" and "knew"), whereas the rest vary the syllable count ("carolings" and "things," "sound" and "around," "air" and "unaware"). Again, whereas the first rhyme uses two nouns ("carolings" and "things"), the others rely on different parts of speech: noun and adjective ("sound" and "around," "air" and "unaware"), preposition and verb ("through" and "knew"). Few readers are likely to say, "Hey, 'through' and 'knew' are monosyllables, but at least they're different parts of speech!" And it doesn't seem likely that the poet sat chewing his pen tip and thinking, "Okay, time for a two-syllable word to rhyme with 'sound.' " What Corn is showing here is that informed half-awareness makes for writing so fluid that the poet hides his tricks even from himself.

After nine chapters on stanza, refrain, syllable-count verse, and other aspects of formalism, Corn devotes his final chapter to what he calls "unmetered poetry," where, we might assume, informed half-awareness slips into blissful ignorance as the unschooled poet, probably thinking of himself as a rebel against past tyrannies, scribbles his unmusical prose, his line not weaving back and forth smartly like the shuttle of that loom described in chapter 1 but moseying around the page like a calf who has found a gap in the fence of traditional prosody. Well, not on Alfred Corn's ranch: "Those who have made a close study of traditional prosody usually write better unmetered poems than those who haven't," he opines, "acknowledging regular patterns by making intelligent departures from them." And "if we say we are writing 'unmetered poetry,' the implication is that we are nevertheless acquainted with the body of poems written in syllable-stress meter, to which the new method has a discoverable relationship."

This dispassionate language veers dangerously close to the cliff-edge of value judgment—that little word "new" is a loaded one, but more on that later—and the reader would not be wrong, I think, in assuming that, from Corn's viewpoint, the calf that strays too far into free-verse territory is likely to disappear in the uncharted waste. Perhaps surprisingly, then, the chapter (and the book) ends with a debunking of the common objections opposed camps make to both unmetered and metered poetry and a celebration of this century's rich trove of poems composed in both manners: among the unmetered, work by Whitman, Stevens, Moore, Auden, Langston Hughes, Plath and so on; among the metered, poems by Frost, Robert Penn Warren, Walcott, Clampitt, Hacker, and Gioia. Corn is a much-published poet himself, and both his metrical and unmetered poetry illustrate how skillfully he practices the preachments he offers others in this slender, handsome, informative volume.

To go from Corn to Hartman is not a move straight down, exactly, but a peculiar, angled decline. Hartman's subject is not traditional prosody per se (though prosody figures significantly); instead, it is what he describes as the "cyber-partnership" between himself and a group of increasingly sophisticated computer programs designed to write poetry. The key concept, at least in the early chapters of *Virtual Muse,* is "juxtaposition," the modernist implications of which I assume Hartman derives from Roger Shattuck's brilliant *The Banquet Years: The Origins of the Avant-Garde in France, 1885 to World War I,* which argues that the classical tradition is built on the principle of transition, in which one idea leads logically to another, whereas modernism owes its essential character to juxtaposition, in which ideas are placed next to each other and the logic of the placement, if any, is to be worked out in the mind of the beholder. The example I use to explain this difference to students is this: classical art is the British Museum, with the halls laid out in good order and the objects lined up chronologically, whereas modern art is the British Museum after a World War I bomb hits it and everything gets blown into the air and comes to earth in a new, random relationship, in which case the British Museum is no longer itself but something like Eliot's *Waste Land.*

The beholder of this new artistic landscape, in Hartman's case, is himself, and the juxtaposition is done by his computer, which he has programmed to cobble words and phrases together, much as Eliot might have hired a hardworking assistant to pick through the rubble of Western civilization and come up with some likely fragments for the master to assemble in final form. In doing so, Hartman is combating the tired stereotype of science as poetry's opposite and replacing it with an approach championed by thinkers like Lewis Carroll (whose "'Twas brillig, and the slithy toves / Did gyre and gimble in the wabe," Hartman suggests, makes more sense than a first glance suggests) and Ferdinand de Saussure (whose idea that language is a "structure of differences" means that words take their meaning, not from their relation to the things they describe, but from their relation to, and, mainly, their differences from, other words). From Carroll to Saussure to a computer, then, whose binary chatter might make no more sense than "Jabberwocky"—ask a computer what it's thinking, says Hartman, and it will reply something like 11010001011110101100101010—but from those "bits and pieces" we might just derive "grand structures of meaning."

One of Hartman's early assistants in the search for grand structures was a computer program named Travesty. (In an area of human endeavor largely devoid of humor—prosody, I mean, not computers—Hartman gets extra points for irony.) Travesty takes an "input text," such as a passage from Ecclesiastes, and turns it into an "output text," which can range from gobbledygook to something that actually sounds literary. On the one hand, as Hartman says, "We can reduce Dr. Johnson to inarticulate imbecility, make Shakespeare talk very thickly through his hat, or exhibit Francis Bacon laying waste his own edifice of logic"; on the other, "we can watch sense evolve and meaning stagger up onto its own miraculous feet," sharing the sense of wonder "that James Joyce aimed at in the 'Oxen of the Sun' chapter of *Ulysses,* where the history of the language from grunts to Parliamentary orations unfolds like a morality play before our ears."

These are heady thoughts, but describing a grand structure of meaning is one thing and building it another. Of "Monologues of Soul and Body," the fifteen-page poem co-authored with Travesty, perhaps the best that can be said is what Hartman himself says: "In the end, I read nonsense all day for several long days; and when I couldn't read any more, I stuck with the best I'd found." Apparently, this includes lines like

> The che seter. Island re sposevelogypt Moorphoted
> asking on moring toweirtournateen O'Rostionce a
> gothe pairs in—trare fich me sposer of and res.

Actually, the whole poem isn't all that awful; there are enough interesting topics—war, chess, history, Rossini, the mathematician Alan Turing—to give it some coherence, and enough variety to the forms of the different parts—prose, short poems, longer stanzaic ones—to impart a sense of freshness. In the end, though, the whole adds up intellectually, to some extent, though never emotionally. But since computers don't have emotions, how could we expect them to be helpful in this way? "Monologues of Soul and Body" is the kind of poem more likely to elicit a "Hmmm, interesting" than a "Wow!"

The same is true for the other poems Hartman writes with the assistance of other computer programs: a metrical poem, a prose poem, a "Talmudic" or Bakhtinian poem with multiple voices. Hartman is an engaging autobiographer, and *Virtual Muse* is great fun to read. (Like all savvy memoirists, Hartman knows you'll never go broke making fun of yourself, as he does when recalling an early botched attempt at a metrical poem and reflects, "Dr. Moreau, too, in the horror story by H. G. Wells, got his beasts to walk on two legs.") But when I read the seven computer poems in the appendix, I couldn't muster much more than a "Hmmm, interesting" each time.

In his concluding chapter, called "Unconclusion," Hartman accounts for the distance I felt from these poems when he writes, "One effect of computer poetry experiments is usually to release language from contingency." Oh, dear: the "c" word, used as anathema by Language Poets more interested in reducing Dr. Johnson to inarticulate imbecility or making Shakespeare talk thickly through his hat than in writing poems that engage the intellect and the emotions not only monumentally but simultaneously. I'm happy that Lewis Carroll's slithy toves did gyre and gimble in the wabe, so happy that I don't ever need them to do it again. Good poets always release words from contingency just by using them in startling new relations to other words, and the poems in *Virtual Muse* suggest that computers can't do anything that an experienced, impassioned, and word-drunk poet can't do better.

If Alfred Corn's *The Poem's Heartbeat* were a person, it would be a sort of priestly, older-brother schoolmaster, adept in several literatures and devoted to poetry in all its forms. Hartman's *Virtual Muse* would probably look something like Robocop, a biomechanical marvel more likely to inspire awe than admiration. And Derek Attridge's *Poetic Rhythm* anthropomorphized would be that high-school teacher you resented but now treasure, the one in the drip-dry shirt with the pocket protector who taught you typing or some other rote skill. *Poetic Rhythm* has many virtues, and, like the Corn and Hartman books, moments of engaging folksiness, such as Attridge's argument that we are all innately skilled at prosody as shown by the fact that any two-year-old can correctly chant

> Star light, star bright,
> First star I see tonight,
> I wish I may, I wish I might,
> Have the wish I wish tonight

with its ploddingly slow first light line, its high-speed third line, and the other two that fall between these extremes with cadences of their own. He also demonstrates how metrical practice has been loosened and tightened over the ages, with Chaucer's regular meters giving way to a period of highly irregular verse, which was succeeded by an era of strict regularity in the mid-sixteenth century only to be followed by the innovations of Spenser and Shakespeare and the even greater ones of Donne and Milton. Regularity came back in fashion with Dryden and Pope, and then the Romantics ushered in the final loosening of meters and the new search for forms that is still under way and includes everything from the experimental metrics of Browning and Hopkins to the radical retooling of the conventional poetic line by Whitman.

All this is to say that Attridge covers most of the same ground that Corn does; if he isn't as grounded as Corn is in other literatures, he more than makes up for it in pedagogic thoroughness with the exercises and chapter summaries that suggest that *Poetic Rhythm* is meant for a classroom of beginners. Though I'm not sure that getting an 87 on a quiz on "duple syllable-stress verse" will have you writing like Shelley, this book could be quite useful in the hands of a teacher who knows what he or she is doing.

And so, as we wipe the chalk dust from our hands and end up getting it all over our clothes anyway, we leave Attridge's classroom to board the boat that took Marlow to Mistah Kurtz. To complete the anthropomorphosis of these four books, *The Scissors of Meter* is, in the end, Kurtz himself, and the reader is Marlow, putt-putting upriver to the Inner Station, where he finds the final truth, the final madness. I knew I'd be seeing heads on stakes soon when I read on the first page that "the radical lack of a strong theory of meter, which is the greatest part of prosody and which I take as standing for prosody in this book, has made prosodic scholarship arcane, unfashionable, indeed *impossible* in the sense of offering a place from which theory as such might be ruthlessly criticized" (emphasis Donald Wesling's). And the heads are those of traditional prosodists. For Wesling says later that "traditional metrics massacres reality and reconstitutes it in a drastically simplified model; it purchases universal rules at a cost of excessive narrowness" and then, improbably, "grammetrics in my version seeks relational propositions that show the interaction of metrical and grammatical segments of several sizes, and that lead in turn to interpretive hypotheses; it snatches wealth from the jaws of indefeasibility."

There's always wealth at the end of the river, we've heard; that's why we keep steaming along, even though the landscape is getting increasingly bizarre. And then, when we arrive at the Inner Station, we find there's no big payoff anyway. Because the basic idea of grammetrics is not all that difficult: it's to show how, not merely meter, but the intersection of grammar and meter create a poem's sense, or, as Wesling says, how "interference of grammatical and metrical systems creates, and arcs over to the reader, cognitive energy." In English, normal grammar consists of subject, verb, and object, and normal meter consists of stressed and unstressed syllables in patterned alternation. These two norms and their variants can either collide or collude, so that we might get a poetic line made up of a "normal sentence, normal meter" but also "normal sentence, exceptional meter," and so on. This kind of analysis is not going to work on "concrete poetry, talk poetry of the sort David Antin practices, and Ashbery-like postmodern writing," but it will work on, say, Shakespeare's sonnet "Th'Expense of Spirit," which grammetrics reveals to be either a hating or self-hating and certainly a failed attempt to define lust, a poem of *"frustrated definition,"* as it were (again, Wesling's emphasis).

But we knew that already. The poem is used effectively to illustrate how grammetrics works—Shakespeare's meter wrenches words from context and creates peculiar emphases—but grammetrics tells us nothing new about the poem. Grammetrics itself may not be all that new: Wesling lists a group of scholars he admires, smart folks who think the way he does and who "write analyses in a more or less grammetrical manner," and then asks "why other readers do not talk this way about what they read is a wholly separate study, a sociology of scholarship." Well, they don't talk that way because their heads are on stakes, lopped off by *The Scissors of Meter.*

To follow the river of prosody all the way to the Inner Station is to end up in a country so obsessed with meter that it overlooks everything else in poetry, which is considerable. If you stand nervously on the prow of the boat and look only for the first signs of Kurtz's empire, you might miss that kid on the bank who's skipping stones across the water. Some of the stones the kid throws land just a few feet away, sending up an impressive rooster tail of water and then vanishing, while others splash only a couple of times and sink. But some stones skip six, seven, eight times, the way they're supposed to. Ping, ping, ping: they disappear in the darkness that swallows the water, the opposite bank, the woods beyond. The kid's a freeverser, maybe one of Whitman's bastard offspring that he bragged about, and therefore a bit of a risk-taker, and some of the risks don't pay off, although some of the seeming clunkers are actually deliberate change-ups intended to vary the rhythm of the skips or at least provide a little relief to that shoulder which aches like a son of a gun, yeah, though it's worth it to finally make that one perfect toss and hear that one stone splash off into the distance, ever more faintly.

It's not really the job of any of those books to go beyond the boundaries that their titles suggest. But there is, after all, that whole tradition that begins with the Bible and comes up through Blake and Whitman and Ginsberg and is responsible for most of the poems being written today: not "free verse" in the sense of chopped-up prose but variations on the Old Testament–based Hebrew poetry shaped by the repetition of, not stressed and unstressed syllables, but parallel ideas.

This parallelism, this skipping of words across the page like stones skipped on water, takes three forms. It is synonymous when the original and the subsequent thoughts are identical; antithetical when the original and subsequent thoughts contrast; and synthetic when the one is developed or enriched by the other.

Here, for example, is an example of synonymous parallelism from "Song of Myself":

> I celebrate myself, and sing myself,
> And what I assume you shall assume,
> For every atom belonging to me as good belongs to you.

And antithetical parallelism:

> A child said *What is the grass?* fetching it to me with full hands;
> How could I answer the child? I do not know what it is any more than
> he.

And synthetic parallelism:

> Do I contradict myself?
> Very well then I contradict myself,
> (I am large, I contain multitudes.)

This too is a kind of formal poetry, though it's not metered. And not to make more of it, either in the books under consideration or in this essay, is like saying that Germany is Turkey because a lot of Turks live there.

In addition to English metrics and the Old Testament–style parallelism championed by Blake, Whitman, Ginsberg, and their adherents, there is another poetic tradition that is separate from these two though capable of working with either. This tradition begins roughly with the French symbolists (Mallarmé, Verlaine, Rimbaud, and the Jules Laforgue whose *vers libre* struck a chord with Eliot and Pound) and was extended and enriched in this century by the work of the surrealists and the thinking of Freud and Jung. Probably most poetry being written these days takes into account

the parallelism of Hebrew poetry or the dream imagery of the symbolists or both, and a poet-in-training needs to learn as much about
these traditions as the English metrical one.

Or maybe not. Even Wesling, the most theoretical of our four
theoreticians, says that "lack of an adequate metrical theory has
never prevented the writing of poems." (He might have mentioned
that, in his consulting room, Freud kept in plain view the words
of his French master, Jean-Martin Charcot: "La théorie, c'est bon,
mais ça n'empêche pas d'exister"; as far as that goes, theory n'empêche pas d'écrire la poésie, either.) Wesling also quotes Georges
Duhamel and Charles Vildrac, who wrote, in *Notes sur la technique
poétique* (1910), "Le poète doit plus de confiance à son oreille qu'à
l'Institut phonétique. . . . Mais d'abord il faut être un poète." My
English translation would be, "The poet ought to have more confidence in his ear than in the Phonetic Institute. . . . But first he
needs to be a poet."

But doesn't it sound better in French? Because it's in another
language, we'll never be able to reproduce the precise sense of
Duhamel and Vildrac's original intention, but that's okay, because
we're talking about poetry here, not science, and far from being
harmed by lacunae and uncertainties, poetry is actually helped by
them. In critiquing Coleridge's famous definition of poetry as "the
best words in the best order," Charles O. Hartman correctly notes
that this makes the poet's job one of judgment rather than creation,
and creation relies on a certain incompleteness to succeed.

Hartman also quotes Wallace Stevens's statement that "poetry
must resist the intelligence almost successfully," which is a model
of aesthetics similar to that argued in Wolfgang Iser's *The Act of
Reading*. According to Iser, the writer leaves a "fundamental asymmetry" when he finishes a poem, and then the reader fills in the
empty parts and creates a symmetry. The art of reading takes place
on a playing field defined by boredom on one side and overstrain

on the other, to use Iser's terms, and the successful poem is located somewhere between those two boundaries.

To write that poem, the poet needs to know many things—everything Alfred Corn has to say in *The Poem's Heartbeat*, bits and pieces from the other three books, more about Old Testament parallelism and French symbolism—although the knowledge of many things does not guarantee the production of great poetry. Probably it would help if the poet has a respect or at least a tolerance for all the poetic traditions and does not merely believe, as Robert Pinsky has said, that free verse is written out of grief for the meters it does not use. (As that big crybaby Walt Whitman would say, I hear America weeping.) Before going to work, the poet should begin every day by having breakfast with the Cumaean Sibyl. But if he only writes like her, we'll end up with stale riddles instead of fresh poems.

Don't Know Much about History

SAMENESS VERSUS ORIGINALITY IN POETRY

1. MORE THAN A LITTLE IRRITATED

Recently, some students involved in Campus Entertainment asked me to open for former-punk-chanteuse-now-spoken-word performer Lydia Lunch. So on the appointed night I go to the little club located in the Student Union and walk into the green room, and there's Lydia Lunch, looking more than a little irritated. I'd wanted to introduce myself as a fellow artiste, so I had with me a signed copy of the collection of mine I was going to read from, *Big-Leg Music.* I introduce myself and present the book, which she glances at and sets aside. In an attempt to break the brittle silence, I say, "Well, um, let's see: Ms. Lunch, how would you describe yourself?" And Lydia Lunch says, "I'm a confrontationalist a woman who acts like a man I'm pro-pornography I'm anti-censorship because pornography doesn't humiliate women it humiliates men they're always searching for that magic fucking golden elixir called pussy!!"

And that's just green-room chatter: on stage, and after I've read my three little milquetoast poems, Lydia Lunch starts shouting fuck this and fuck that and fuck all my ex-boyfriends and all Republicans and pretty much everybody, really. Not that she singled me out for abuse personally, but then she never winked at me or mouthed the words, "Not you, Dave."

2. "OUR POETS CAN WHIP YOUR POETS' ASSES"

Lydia Lunch's work is not included in *The Outlaw Bible of American Poetry*, which is odd considering there are two photos of her in the book, both capturing the curled-lip sneer that is her trademark. Yet her spirit hovers over its pages. A snotty kid myself once, I was prepared to like the desperadoes of literature whose *oeuvre* is collected in these pages, but, like Lydia Lunch, they made it clear from the get-go that they can't stand me. From a press release that says "American poetry was never about academia" to the editor's introductory "Our poets can whip your poets' asses," this Bible is proffered by Kaufman and his fellow brigands the way the other Bible is offered by a Southern Baptist or the Koran by the Taliban brotherhood: it's the way, the truth, and the light, and if you don't agree, then it's off with your hands in the village square.

Again and again, the outlaw poets claim Walt Whitman as their god. Kaufman even includes a section of "Song of the Open Road" that ends with these lines:

> They pass, I pass, anything passes, none can be interdicted,
> None but are accepted, none but shall be dear to me.

But it's the nature of fundamentalism to distort the words of the scripture-giver, to say that Christ would interpret the Second Amendment to mean all Americans should carry assault weapons or that Allah wants women to be illiterate stay-at-homes.

Predictably, these Shi'ite bohos who rail against what they see as the sameness of "academic poetry" (whatever that is) practice a numbing sameness in their writing. Typically, the poems of *The Outlaw Bible* are skinny, unpunctuated, and fragmented, though their worst feature is their unvarying tendency not to end effectively but to simply stop. It's as though the writer—who has been too bored to take any care with the body of the poem—is saying, "Let's just end it here, folks."

Poet Mike Topp introduces his work by saying "I don't really like the Western idea of creativity, with its emphasis on originality and the insistence that everyone must be so interested in what the poet is thinking." Fair enough, Mike! The other petty thieves and litter-bugs of *The Outlaw Bible* seem to agree; like you, no doubt they'd endorse the ethos expressed in Mike Golden's "Write a Fucking Poem," reproduced here in its entirety:

> Write a fucking poem
>
> every fucking time
> you don't know what to do.
> You'll have a body of work
> despite yourself.

Well, you can't say he doesn't practice what he preaches.

Not all the poems in *The Outlaw Bible* are as lazy and cynical as this one, of course. Not all of them are poems, as far as that goes: a lot of them are song lyrics by Bob Dylan, Woody Guthrie, Patti Smith, and Tom Waits, which, in the absence of music, means they are performance scripts rather than poems. In fact, almost every piece in this book is a script for a performance; it's probably a lot of fun to hear Sapphire, referred to in the introduction as "the reign-ing queen of American letters" (oh, I doubt it), read "Wild Thing," but on the page, her words are lifeless.

There are a fair number of poems by celebrity nonpoets like James Dean as well as nonsong lyric "poems" by Jim Morrison, who, along with Charles Bukowski and Jewel, is one third of the dark triumvirate whose evil influence is pervasive in American un-dergraduate poetry these days. (A wonderful rock 'zine called *One Shot* went out of business several years ago, its editor told me, be-cause he couldn't stand to get one more poem about the death of the Lizard King.) And there are actually some real writers here:

Allen Ginsberg, Victor Hernández Cruz, Henry Miller, Gregory
Corse, Rudolfo Anaya, Ishmael Reed, Ai, Joy Harjo, and others who
write work that stands on its own. But 90 percent of these poets
come across as simply depressed—too depressed to work very hard
on their poetry. These lines from Ferrucio Brugnaro's "Buy, Always Consume" (translated by Jack Hirschman) stand for both the
sophomoric attitudes and the disdain for craftsmanship expressed
throughout:

> Buy, always buy
>   carry home
>   more than you can carry;
>   consume, consume,
>   sink, sink into the shit,
>   shit shit shit.

You could say these are timeless lines because they're not anchored
to any particular context, but that's the problem: they're timeless
in a bad way, because they just hang in the air. It's too bad some
lines by Lydia Lunch weren't included, after all. She, at least, seems
to have read someone beside herself; the Marquis de Sade and
Georges Bataille, for example, are major influences, and her work
is the better for it. Maybe that's the problem. Maybe the ornery
cusses who edited *The Outlaw Bible* figured that their filly had just
a little too much book-larnin'.

The poems in *An American Mosaic* are the product of a Nashville
workshop for homeless men and women. Self-examination is the
theme here; wistfulness takes the place of the street bravado of
The Outlaw Bible. That pitches the poetry at about the same grade
level—most of the poems in both books could have been written
by tenth-graders at a good alternative school—but this time it's the
sad kids who're writing, not the mad ones.

Here are some typical lines from a poet who may as well remain
nameless (why rub it in?):

> So I will keep on caring
> Taking the pain you give . . .
> Because I know, my darling,
> Without you I could not live.
>
> *"Sometimes You Hurt Me Terribly"*

The workshop leaders might have pointed out that, first of all, not
every intense feeling makes for a good poem. They could have said
that tick-tock rhymes are boring and juvenile, that inverting the
syntax to make such rhymes only compounds the error. And certainly they should have told the poet that nobody likes a sniveler,
no matter how justifiable the sniveling. (And since they were either
unable or unwilling to give her sound poetic advice, one hopes they
at least had the decency to shout, "Lose the boyfriend, honey!")

Rebel Yell, whose real name is Lori Lee, is the best poet in *An
American Mosaic;* her work is out of Whitman via early Kenneth
Koch:

> And When I Was Sleeping in Alabama, Where A Group Got Started
> Singing Their Song And Looking At The Spanish Moss That Draped
> on The Tall Cedar Trees, The Heart of Dixieland.
>
> And Looking At The Old Mansion Of the South And Hearing
> Ghostly Music Inside The Dunleith Mansion, Where Miss Percy
> Could Still Be Heard Playing A Harp Only At Dusk. ("What Really
> Happened to Us")

Again, though, Ms. Yell's workshop instructors let her down: all
her poems here look exactly the same, which means they appear
gimmicky and monotonous.

In the end, none of the *American Mosaic* poets deliver, probably
because they weren't asked to. The crime is not that they wrote but
that they were published. Their instructors allowed them to make

craft secondary to personal expression, and if that was the goal of the workshop, the process should have stopped there.

Fortunately, the *American Mosaic* poets will not have a significant readership. The *Outlaw Bible* poets will do better in this respect. The nose-thumbing at academe notwithstanding, this anthology, like almost all poetry collections, will sell well only if it is adopted widely as a course text. And since the majority of poetry classes are taught by nonpoets, *The Outlaw Bible* looks like a good choice for an instructor who doesn't want to work very hard and keep the kids happy. Besides, *The Outlaw Bible* purports to be rebellious, and rebellion sells. Unfortunately for *An American Mosaic*, self-pity is not big at the box office.

What's largely missing from both books is a sense of history: not the Edict of Nantes or Diet of Worms kind but the history of other people, what they've thought and how they've felt from the beginning of time through yesterday. Without this perspective, the poet's materials seem dazzling in their freshness; with it, the poet can pick and choose, discarding the trite and recognizing the truly new for what it is. If Mike Topp really doesn't like originality, he must be happy with the kind of poetry gathered in these two books. It's yawningly unoriginal; what's worse is that none of the poets or editors seems to have noticed that it is.

3. A MIND LIVELY AND AT EASE

I was no more than three lines into the title poem of *Like Most Revelations* when I thought, if Richard Howard had drawn up the plans for the battle of Waterloo, publicans would now be pushing Côtes du Rhône instead of lager across the bar as they shout "Hurry up, please, it's time!" and Molière would be hailed as the world's greatest playwright, not that nobody from Stratford-on-Avon. Anomalous thought, yes, not exactly the sort of judgment of which literary criticism is usually made, but certainly the kind of idea that comes to mind when one is reading imaginative writing, the best of which is made of and therefore likely to engender precisely such fancies. The poem begins:

> It is the movement that incites the form,
> discovered as a downward rapture—yes,
> it is the movement that delights the form,
> sustained by its own velocity.

The remaining three quatrains are built around variants on the first and third lines of this one: "it is the movement that delays the form" and "it is the movement that betrays the form"; then "it is the movement that deceives the form" and "it is the movement that achieves the form"; and, finally, "it is the movement that negates the form" and "it is the movement that creates the form." That, I thought to myself, is strategy; it is a plan that is flexible and surprising and that ultimately transcends itself. It is a big statement contained in a small field. As for the military metaphor, although it's not fashionable to say so in some circles, every poet I know wants to conquer his or her readers, all of whom, and this too is less than politically correct in certain venues, have presented themselves precisely for the purpose of being conquered; otherwise they wouldn't have presented themselves at all. And the French win, in this case, because Howard, who has published over 150 translations of works by Cioran, Stendhal, and Barthes (including, most recently, *The Charterhouse of Parma*), is so ardent a francophile.

More important, though, than either the military or French aspect of my metaphor is its historical nature. You have to know history to know Howard. And if you don't (and you're not likely to know as much as he does), he'll teach it to you. The majority of the poems in *Like Most Revelations* are either Browning-style monologues, usually in the voices of rather discriminating speakers, or else Howard's reflections on these types—your Baudelaires, your Austens, your Becketts, your Mark Strands—the sorts of people who probably wouldn't mind ruling the world if it weren't such a bother. The book is an extended conversation with the Great Fastidious Dead (and, to a lesser extent, their living heirs).

An example of one such speaker, a personage undeniably elevated, exigent, and extinct, is the one in "Poem Beginning with a Line by Isadora Duncan," a pretty treatise on the pleasures of denial, especially its utility as a tool of conquest: *"The third time I resisted D'Annunzio / was after the war,"* she begins, confiding in the following stanzas the circumstances of her other successful demolishings of his "erectile tendencies." The details are amusing, yes, but they're only made possible by scrupulous mental bookkeeping, for, as the speaker says, "counting was / a crucial part of it."

There is a consistent treatment of experience withheld in *Like Most Revelations.* The more that is withheld, of course, the more there is to think and write about, making it altogether appropriate to meditate on "Baudelaire's list / of *petits poèmes en prose* / projected and not written: 'Captive in a Lighthouse,' 'Festival / in a Deserted City' " ("Undertakings") and Beckett's "missing links between / inscription and erasure" ("Homage"). Howard is our most Jamesian of poets, the one who sees most clearly that literature is made less of what we do than what we don't do and think about instead. James, of course, was our most Austenian of novelists, and the prime quality of her outlook is also that of his, Howard's, and most of the speakers in the poems in this collection, a quality best defined in a brief statement by Austen quoted in "For David Kalstone, 1932–86": "A mind lively and at ease can do / with seeing nothing, and can see nothing / that does not answer." The mind lively and at ease may, in fact, prefer nothing to a something that might dull or perturb it.

"Historical," "Jamesian": already two tags have been applied to Howard's work that would cause the eyes of the average sophomore to glaze over and might make even the most effete reader wonder if Howard isn't promoting here a kind of eat-your-spinach poetry. But Howard's history and his Jamesian scenarios are shot through with generous lacings of leavening puns and epigrams:

he refers to D'Israeli as a "Jew *d'esprit*" ("A Beatification") and reminds readers that "Jesus said / Forgive our enemies—nothing about our friends" ("For Matthew Ward, 1951–90"); he states *"Plus ça change, plus c'est la même pose"* ("Theory of Flight: 1908") and, in defiance of the religious right, "buggers / *can* be choosers" ("For David Kalstone, 1932–86").

Given Howard's extensive range of learned references, not to mention what seems to have been and continues to be an absolutely fabulous social calendar (his Rolodex must be in multiple editions by now), one of the pleasures of reading him is to come across so many people who aren't canonical or otherwise historically embalmed. Naturally he would be drawn to the poetry of Mark Strand, he whose much-anthologized "Keeping Things Whole" begins "In a field / I am the absence / of field"; Howard describes Strand (in "Writing Off") as being "content, if not resolved, to be missing / in action, missing in passion— / forsaking as a form of *being there*!" The poem continues its examination of an art founded on the decision to "live on nothing" for five pages and then ends:

> . . . yet the wasted splendor of an empty
>   lot in East Los Angeles
> redefines the state of the art: how much
>   of the world's making was never
> intended for human eyes! Luxor, Lascaux,
>
> sacred places where we learn we can change
>   our faith without changing gods (and
> vice versa) . . . To which I add the image
>   of an unvisitable shrine
> where obscure artisans have succeeded
>
> in transcending the five destinies
>   by which we claim to be guided:

mind body nation language home. This is
how we learn, by just such unseen
art, to approach the divine.

Strand, of course, is the great untoothpaste ad of our day, the great
noncheerleader, the ultimate anti-salesman. What Disney and Mc-
Donald's and Coca-Cola are for, he is aggressively indifferent to—
if he were a shopping-mall movie theater, he'd be a nihilplex, and
Howard would be his cashier, tearing the tickets *before* they're sold.
To both, that which we cannot see is sacred, and it's the unvisitable
shrines that are the holiest.

Indeed, many of the characters in these poems appear just as
heroically reticent, their very reluctance a badge of honor. Consider
just two excerpts that stand for a dozen others:

> Many of us, inexorably
> subservient to your cool evasions,
>   found them more flattering than candor
> could ever be.
>
>   *"And Tell Sad Stories"*

and

> Your own maneuvers you confined to
>   the background—more room there than up front
> where the young struggle and sweat for their applause.
>
>   *"For Robert Phelps, Dead at 66"*

The revelations in *Like Most Revelations* are really one revelation:
the more the artist conceals, the more, as the title poem says, he
beguiles our attention.

Howard's next collection of poems, *Trappings,* is a practical application of the hypothesis that is *Like Most Revelations.* If that book
argues that the most precious is the least seen, this one tests that

idea, chasing it through history's shadows with flashlight and butterfly net. As before, Howard favors either the dramatic monologue or its cousin, the poem in which an observer tracks the would-be speaker across the stage of his or her life, intuiting what he or she might be thinking. But here what is said or thought is that much more concrete than in the earlier book. For example, in "Avarice, 1849: A Distraction," Nadar and Balzac discuss the deceptiveness of photography and fiction—by extension, any art. The paradox is that the one artist is practicing his art on the other, who agrees that the photo isn't really himself, though he tries to buy it anyway. Perhaps Balzac would agree with the speaker in "For Mona Van Duyn, Going On," who says that we are precisely because of "our continual tendency not to be"; as our various selves flash into being and then as quickly recede into the dark out of which we've just stepped and to which we'll soon return, perhaps a photographic portrait is as good an illusion of permanence as any.

But whereas another poet might treat our love of solidity as self-defeating, even tragic, Howard is amused by the idea. Many of his poems (in all of his books) are funny, and all but a few are witty in the dual and inseparable senses of both "comic" and "inventive." For example, anyone who has ever wondered what it was like to have been the emissary who has to listen to the simpering murderer describing his last duchess in Browning's celebrated poem will feel a smile coming on upon reading "Nikolaus Mardruz to His Master Ferdinand, Count of Tyrol, 1565." Mardruz is a younger Polonius, talky yet brimming with good counsel. He knows what's up, he loves his young charge, and, above all, he's loyal to his master, so he brokers a deal whereby the young woman's dowry will not only drip into the duke's coffers by degrees ("say, one fifth each year") but also double after that time, "always assuming / that Her Grace enjoys / her usual smiling health." Further, Mardruz posits that Ferrara will be "her last Duke" and that there is even a "next Duke" waiting in the wings in the form of a certain "young

lordling." Howard turns the tables on the mean old nobleman in
this rejoinder. We may know better—may know that the deserving will always be trounced by rich autocrats—but Howard writes
what we want to be true, not what is. Reading this poem, we are
like Balzac clutching the portrait that portrays him as he wishes
to be rather than as he is, for we bite into the fruit of hope, not
knowledge.

Indeed, poem after poem in *Trappings* is a gift sent to us out of
history's dark, and Howard is as often as not a messenger bringing
us something that we didn't know, something that, "true" or not,
we are glad to have. A five-poem suite with the amusing (there he
goes again) title of "Family Values" deals with the lifestyle of those
zany Miltons, blind poet John and daughters Deborah, Anne, and
Mary. Together they recall an earlier family from English literature, the Lears: papa John has his own way of doing things, and
while Deborah and Anne are go-along-get-along types, mouthy
Mary is feisty and independent:

> . . . Let my sisters
> wear the red slippers even as they take
> down the words of Eve. It shall not be
> seen by *my* hand that she rhymes with *deceive*.

That makes her the more interesting speaker and thus the focal
point of the suite. But the poems aren't limited to her or even the
family per se, because the last two poems deal with nineteenth-
and twentieth-century painters' representations of Milton dictating to his daughters. Typically, Howard doesn't leave history historical but brings it forward into our time.

And, as in *Like Most Revelations,* personal history parallels the
textbook kind. There are poems here about a younger Howard's
nervous interview with an outspokenly homophobic André Breton
("The Job Interview") and an older one's relations with the dying Muriel Rukeyser, who gives him a computer on which are left

words he makes into the poem he calls "A Sibyl of 1979." Paradoxically, all this actuality in no way inhibits the mind's ability to range freely. Far from calcifying thought by limiting it to known data, Howard's grasp of history seems so sweeping and complete that it leaves us with a sense not only of the fair amount we know but also the even greater amount we don't. And it is in those shadows and lacunae that the mind is at its most fertile play.

4. "UPWARD TOWARD"

WRIGHT: As I look back on [my three trilogies, *Country Music, The World of Ten Thousand Things,* and an as-yet untitled gathering that will include *Chickamauga* and two of the collections under review here, *Black Zodiac* and *Appalachia*], the whole thing seems to be a kind of searching. A kind of movement, if not a narrative, an emotionally organized movement, in an ascending path.

SUAREZ: What do you mean by "an ascending path"?

WRIGHT: Ascending path. Going upward.

SUAREZ: Upward toward? . . .

WRIGHT: Upward toward. Being a secular person, I don't know what it's going upward toward.

(Ernest Suarez, *Southbound: Interviews with Southern Poets*)

Richard Howard's characters seem to step out at the reader from a world that has always been there; the characters emerge from that world and go back to it when the poem is over. Charles Wright, on the other hand, moves across the blank page (and in his poems he is the only character) and, as he moves, makes a world that vanishes the moment he does. He is not particularly attracted to the idea of permanence and instead seems to prefer or at least to be drawn to the mutable.

Thus "Apologia Pro Vita Sua," the first poem in his Pulitzer Prize–winning collection *Black Zodiac* (which is the penultimate book in the last of his "trilogy of trilogies," of which more later), includes these lines:

> How like the past the clouds are,
> Building and disappearing along the horizon,
> Inflecting the mountains,
> > laying their shadows under our feet
>
> For us to cross over on.

If that's the theory—that history doesn't stand still any more than nature does—the poem is dense with little examples of change, such as this one:

> One summer, aged 16, I watched—each night, it seemed—my
> > roommate,
> A college guy, gather his blanket up, and flashlight,
> And leave for his rendezvous with the camp cook—
> > he never came back before dawn.
> Some 40 years later I saw him again for the first time
> Since then, in a grocery store, in the checkout line,
> A cleric from Lexington, shrunken and small. Bearded even.
>
> And all these years I'd thought of him, if at all, as huge
> And encompassing,
> Not rabbit-eyed, not fumbling a half-filled brown sack,
> > dry-lipped, apologetic.

To compare Howard's lines to Wright's is to get the feeling that they are two different media: Howard's are the pixels of a dense image that existed before the reader ever saw it, whereas Wright's are the stylus marks on a dime-store magic tablet: lift the plastic film, and all the pretty words disappear. This may be why it is easier

to quote Wright: Howard's lines are always lodged in a context that
has deep roots and wide branches, whereas Wright's float by, like
the leaves and birds his eye is constantly drawn to, and can be taken
in just as easily.

Also, it won't come as a surprise to realize that, whereas Howard
is often happiest responding to the questions history has left unan-
swered, Wright prefers to restate them. Thus, in "Apologia," he
asks:

> What are the determining moments of our lives?
>   How do we know them?
> Are they ends of things or beginnings?
> Are we more or less of ourselves once they've come and gone?

As the interview excerpt that begins this section suggests, there will
be no explicit answers to those queries, though certainly Wright's
poems in the aggregate suggest that the best response to life's im-
ponderables is, at least in his case, (1) an acceptance of the moving
world that, over time, becomes an affection for it and, of course,
(2) an unconditional reliance on the poetry that both parallels the
world's motion and leads to an understanding of it.

Poetry is at the heart of Wright's poetry, not in a mannered or
self-conscious way but as a virtue beyond all others. Thus "Poem
Half in the Manner of Li Ho" begins "All things aspire to weight-
lessness, / some place beyond the lip of language" and ends "We
hang like clouds between heaven and earth, / between something
and nothing, / Sometimes with shadows, sometimes without." Yet
between these wispy phrasings is this parable, visceral and Whit-
manesque:

> Li Ho, the story goes, would leave home
> Each day at dawn, riding a colt, a servant boy
>
>   walking behind him,
> An antique tapestry bag
> Strapped to his back.

> When inspiration struck, Ho would write
> The lines down and drop them in the bag.
> At night he'd go home and work the lines up into a poem,
> No matter how disconnected and loose-leafed they were.
> His mother once said,
> "He won't stop until he has vomited out his heart."

James Dickey once said, "What you have to realize when you write poetry, or if you love poetry, is that poetry is just naturally the greatest goddamn thing that ever was in the whole universe." Take away the profanity, the colloquial syntax, the Southern speech tags and move the idea to ninth-century China, and the result would be essentially what Wright says in the lines above.

Like Richard Howard, Wright sees personal history (organized around family members and small-town life) and world history (especially the artistic and intellectual variety represented by Dante, Walter Raleigh, Gertrude Stein, and the other public figures who appear in these poems) as poetic coins of roughly equal value. Unlike him, Wright gives more space to nature: the self is sizable in Howard and has much to say, whereas the smaller, quieter self in Wright's poems leaves that much more room for the trees and the rivers. Yet he neither hugs the one nor splashes in the other; it's important to remember that the true human condition is one at a distinct distance from the world: "To be separate, to be apart, is to be whole again" ("Meditation on Summer and Shapelessness"). And to be whole is to be in a state in which language is not especially useful: why try to bridge the gap with words when there is no gap to be bridged? Hence phrases in *Black Zodiac* like "What's the use of words" ("Poem Half in the Manner of Li Ho") and "my words embarrass me" ("Disjecta Membra").

This playful antipathy toward language only deepens in *Appalachia*, where it becomes "our common enemy" ("Venetian Dog"). In this collection, as language loses ground, it's literally the ground

itself that replaces it. Nature is the mise-en-scène in *Black Zodiac;*
in *Appalachia,* it is the lead actor:

> Over the Blue Ridge, the whisperer starts to whisper in tongues.
>
> Remembered landscapes are left in me
> The way a bee leaves its sting,
>   hopelessly, passion-placed,
> Untranslatable language.
> Non-mystical, insoluble in blood, they act as an opposite
> To the absolute, whose words are a solitude, and set to music.
>
> All forms of landscape are autobiographical.
>   *"All Landscape Is Abstract, and Tends to Repeat Itself"*

Landscape is autobiography because it calls us back to the essential human condition of a detachment that amounts to a kind of
completion: "A love of landscape's a true affection for regret, I've
found, / Forever joined, forever apart, / outside us yet ourselves"
("Stray Paragraphs in February, Year of the Rat"). Less will always
be more in Wright's worldview: in "Ars Poetica II" he writes, "I
shall die like a cloud, beautiful, white, full of nothingness." Until
that moment, much of life is passed in an in-between state; the
pages of *Appalachia* are riddled with images of a flanked self:

> This is our world, high privet hedge on two sides. . . .
>   *"A Bad Memory Makes You a Metaphysician,*
>   *a Good One Makes You a Saint"*
>
> For us, what indeed, lying like S. Lorenzo late at night
> On his brazier, lit from above by a hole in the sky,
> From below by coals,
>   his arm thrown up,
> In Titian's great altarpiece, in supplication, what indeed?
>   *"Venetian Dog"*

Still, who knows where the soul goes,
Up or down,
>   after the light switch is turned off, who knows?
>   *"All Landscape Is Abstract, and Tends to Repeat Itself"*

Undoing the self is a hard road.
Somewhere alongside a tenderness that's infinite,
I gather, and loneliness that's infinite.
>   *"Ostinato and Drone"*

At times Wright writes like a Platonist, as when he says "We live in two landscapes, as Augustine might have said, / One that's eternal and divine, / and one that's just the back yard." ("Indian Summer II") or when he calls out "Give me the names for things, just give me their real names" ("The Writing Life"). But he writes this way only when he is agitated. When he transcends that in-between state that is ordinary life and finds peace in dissolution, he sounds like the Keats who, dictating his epitaph, described himself as one whose name was writ in water:

I inhabit who I am, as T'ao Ch'ing says, and walk about
Under the mindless clouds.
>   When it ends, it ends. What else?

One morning I'll leave home and never find my way back—
My story and I will disappear together, just like this.
>   *"After Reading T'ao Ch'ing,*
>   *I Wander Untethered Through the Short Grass"*

In other words, he sounds like a prophet, at least in E. M. Forster's definition not of one who predicts the future but who speaks in a high rhetorical mode, like one of the Old Testament authors. The last stanza of the last poem in *Appalachia* reads this way:

Until the clouds stop, and hush.
Until the left hedge and the right hedge,

the insects and short dogs,
The back porch and barn swallows grain-out and disappear.
Until the bypass is blown with silence, until the grass grieves.
Until there is nothing else.

"Opus Posthumous III"

Ecclesiastes, anyone—Job, Jeremiah, Ezekiel? When nature ceases its motion, when differences dissolve and you can't tell one hedge from the other, the story's over.

Wordsworth wanders lonely as a cloud and finds solace in nature, but he is always at the center of his poetry. Wright disappears the way a cloud does, in a way that suits his kind of poetry and, one suspects, himself as well. In the spring 2000 issue of *Southern Review,* when interviewer Ted Genoways notes that Wright appeared uncomfortable at the Pulitzer reception for *Black Zodiac,* Wright replies:

> I want my poetry to get all the attention in the world, but I want to be the anonymous author of *Black Zodiac.* That's impossible to do, I know. Some people love the spotlight; I like the shadows. I like the spotlight on my work, because that's what's important. It's better-looking and younger and wealthier and more articulate. No, I have never liked the spotlight. I have friends who love it and are great at it. Not me. The attention for the book is wonderful. I'm not sure it's gotten me more readers, but I've got more buyers, and that's good. So keep those cards and letters coming to the bookstores. Not me.

Appalachia is said to complete the nine-volume project sometimes referred to in writings on Wright as his "trilogy of trilogies," the first two of which are the three volumes collected in *Country Music* (1982) and those that comprise *The World of Ten Thousand Things* (1990). The 1995 collection *Chickamauga,* along with *Black Zodiac* and *Appalachia*, are said to comprise the final trilogy, yet *Negative Blue* isn't it, exactly. It's a kind of trilogy plus, since it is comprised of the last three published collections but also contains seven additional poems in a group called "North American Bear," poems that, as the jacket copy says, "suggest new directions." They would have to, of course, since Wright all but drowns his book à la Prospero in the final pages of *Appalachia*. Yet he's got more to say, clearly, though how do you say what you have to say when there's no one there to say it?

Chronology can be a cruel mistress, and it's a little unsettling to read *Negative Blue* after having read *Black Zodiac* and *Appalachia*, since one is really taking a step back and beginning with *Chickamauga*, which appeared five years ago. Not that the Charles Wright of that collection is all that different from the one who wrote the later books; poems with titles like "As Our Bodies Rise, Our Names Turn Into Light" and "Absence Inside an Absence" suggest that he was interested even then in dissolution, evanescence, fulfillment through incompletion. Yet more of the poems in *Chickamauga* than in the other books focus on the author's young, less-settled self: the ten-year-old child in "Sprung Narratives," the young man of twenty-three who finds himself in Italy for the first time in "Mid-Winter Snowfall in the Piazza Dante." And there is, if not much more, at least that much more roiling and unease than in the more recent books, for these are the poems of a man whose life is "this shirt I want to take off, / which is on fire" ("Reading Lao Tzu Again in the New Year"). Reading *Chickamauga* after having read *Black Zodiac*, it's not hard to see why the latter won a Pulitzer Prize: the earlier book hints at an unquiet spirit and prescribes a palliative for its ills, and the later one delivers that palliative richly in the form of an acceptance of, even an affection for, impermanence in all its forms, one of which is this poet's poetry itself.

Which may be why, instead of publishing a trilogy proper, Wright publishes in *Negative Blue* a trilogy-plus-seven-poems that

deliberately disrupts the symmetry of a project that would otherwise have a kind of architectural perfection. Wright is often called
Dantesque for his Italian settings, his fierce love of his native land,
and the geometrical order of his lengthy, complex project. Yet the
poems in "North American Bear" are like a wag's graffiti scrawled
on the statue of the Great Personage in the piazza after midnight,
for they say, in effect, "Just kidding, folks—we're not really finished here, after all." Indeed, the first poem in this section, wittily
titled "Step-children of Paradise," asks, in its second line, "where
to begin?" And not only "where" but "who," since the Wright of
Black Zodiac and *Appalachia* disappeared the way clouds do. The
persona in this cluster of poems moves through them as though he
is not there; if the earlier speaker seems barely corporeal, this one
is little more than an outline against the darkness:

> I walk in the chill of the late autumn night
>
> > > like Orpheus,
>
> Thinking my song, anxious to look back,
> My vanished life an ornament, a drifting cloud, behind me,
> A soft, ashen transcendence
> Buried and resurrected once, then time and again.
> The sidewalk unrolls like a deep sleep.
> Above me the stars, stern stars,
> Uncover their faces.
>
> > > No heartbeat on my heels, no footfall.
> > *the title poem to the "North American Bear" section*

Wright has never claimed privileged status for himself or his writing in his poetry, and certainly there is no more-invisible-than-
thou attitude in these new poems. Or if there is, it's offset by two
additional qualities that always seem present in Wright's poetry,
though their proportion varies from poem to poem: a dry wit, often
in the form of a colloquial phrase that startles amidst the more formal and religious-sounding language; and a more or less Buddhist

sense of responsibility, one that evokes the good-wishes approach of the Dalai Lama more than the good-works strategies of Jimmy Carter:

> When the world has disappeared, someone will have to carry us,
> Unseen and nightlong.
>> When the world has disappeared, amigo,
> Somebody's got to pick up the load.
>
> *"Step-children of Paradise"*

I think I know what Wright is doing here. I think that, when a poet reaches a certain point in life, both chronologically as well as in terms of achievement (which, in Wright's case, is towering), he writes as though his next book might be his last. Thus a "sixty-two-year-old, fallow-voiced, night-leaning man" ("North American Bear") might be expected to try for and attain a certain high rhetorical peak in his work. I might as well write importantly, he thinks; if it all stops here, this would be a good place to stop, and if not, well, I'll think of something. Of course, there's no last book except for the final one, as Yogi Berra might say, and surely there is more to come from this distinguished poet who, like the equally distinguished Richard Howard, is at the top of his game, even though the game is far from over.

A key difference between Howard and Wright is the use they make of history. As seen, Howard is history's mole: he burrows deep into the past and pops up in surprising places, caked with the mud of time. Wright, on the other hand, prefers not to bask or revel in history but to simply toss it out by the handful. Often his references to the great ones come in threes: "Thus do we entertain ourselves on hot days, Aldo Buzzi, / Cees Nooteboom, Gustave Flaubert" ("Passing the Morning under the Serenissima," *Appalachia*), he writes, and "St. John of the Cross, say, or St. Teresa of Avila. / Or even St. Thomas Aquinas" ("Cicada Blue," *Appalachia*). Wright doesn't develop history the way Howard does but refers to it the way one might refer, say, to plant names. He's a name-dropper, but he drops names in a natural and easy (as opposed to a nervous and eager) way—he's a name-dropper the way a tree is a leaf-dropper.

Interestingly, Wright refers to Howard by name in the *South-bound* interview; describing his own essentially visual orientation, he says, "My wife reads constantly. That's the way Richard Howard is, too. That's the way a lot of people I admire are. They just read. I don't." This isn't to say he *hasn't* read Flaubert and the various saints, of course. Besides, with that poet-as-prophet voice, Wright comes across as historical despite himself. If Howard restates history, Wright embodies it.

5. A HELLISH RECYCLING OF THE SAME OLD IDEAS

After the show I opened for her, Lydia Lunch takes off like a scalded dog. And when I go back to the green room to get my sweater, I see she's left the copy of *Big-Leg Music* I gave her, so I get it and put it on my shelf back home, making it, along with all the books I have that people have signed for me, the only book I own that I've signed for somebody else, someone who probably sees me as a reactionary anti-woman's-suffrage punk-ass phallocrat misogynist pig like the rest of her enemies, or maybe just someone she couldn't learn anything from, about which she's almost certainly right.

Still, I think Lydia Lunch should have at least tried to get something from *Big-Leg Music*—or not tried, actually, but just read it with an open mind and waited to see if something happened or didn't happen, either way, because if nothing happens, fine, that's the way it is, usually, whereas if something *does* happen—a little light-flash, a little silent firecracker in your brain, then that's just extra. It's a gift, a little present that comes from beyond the narrow dimensions of your own temporal experience.

History is the great gift-giver, of course. If we let it, it'll give us billions of dollars worth of gifts in the course of a lifetime. And these gifts come in the form of choices: what to do and what not to do, sure, but also just what to think about, what to taste, to savor. In very different ways, poets like Richard Howard and Charles Wright are conduits for history—not the history of generals and battles but that of ideas and culture and complex emotions.

Without history, poetry is just a hellish recycling of the same old ideas everybody has all the time. The *American Mosaic* poets have no awareness of history at all, which means that their poems convey sentiments that are stale because they are so familiar. The *Outlaw Bible* poets are a shade better because at least they have some awareness of the tradition in which they're working. They acknowledge Whitman, though they distort his populist message into a grimier-than-thou elitism. And a number of them mention Rimbaud, though one suspects what they're really drawn to is his life rather than his writing. If Rimbaud had stayed home, they probably wouldn't have mentioned him at all.

Is There a Southern Poetry?

1. "ONLY THE POET'S VOICE"

The answer to the question that is the title of this essay is yes, although southern poetry may not be what you think it is—certainly it is not the poetic equivalent of southern fiction. A second question follows closely on the heels of the first: do I care? And the answer to this question is also yes. Yes, you care if there is a southern poetry, even if, and perhaps especially if, you are not a southerner.

These two questions, though, are really the offspring of a larger one: an ur-question, as it were. The ur-question is, what is the big deal about the South, anyway?

This is the big deal: just before I began writing this essay, there was a column in the *New York Times* describing a incident that had occurred a week earlier in Boston. The prime minister of India and his entourage had checked into the Four Seasons Hotel, insisting they be served by whites only. The management had acquiesced, and all parking attendants, bellhops, clerks, maids, and waiters who were of African-, Asian-, or Latin-American descent were reassigned to other tasks and their duties given to Caucasian employees. Hotel employees complained, hotel officials apologized, and the Massachusetts Commission Against Discrimination is investigating. All in all, it was a shameful episode, one the columnist puts into helpful perspective in his lead paragraph, which reads: "It was the kind of ugliness you expected from the South in the 1950s, but it happened last week in one of the great hotels of Boston."

Notice what happens in this sentence. The entire South—not Little Rock or Selma but all eleven states and the people therein— is both derided and put to good use. In the 1950s, the same thing is as likely to have happened in St. Louis or Cleveland or any other place where bullies threw their weight around and cowards knuckled under, but the journalist does not invoke the Midwest or the Great Lakes area. The South, he says, so that Bostonians and New Yorkers can both comprehend and distance themselves from the evil as they look at the northern hotel executives through klan-colored glasses.

After all, the *Times* columnist could have simply described the enormity of the Four Seasons and its "southern"-style management and let the hotel officials dangle from the rope they had prepared for their own hangings. Instead, he took a gratuitous swipe at a few hundred million individuals and did so in a way that confirms a vital truth: that the South is simultaneously at the periphery and the heart of American culture in the way that no other region is.

Put another way, the South is the minority portion that dramatizes the majority. Every day in the United States of America, the South is derided and imitated: its historical image of backwardness, truculence, clannishness, and pig-headed, self-righteous aggression is played out in facets of contemporary life from professional sports to statehouse politics, fashion (*vide* the ubiquitous duck-billed cap), gang warfare, and military policy, just as its image of vampiristic plantation leisure is replicated in debutante balls, "Greek" organizations, the Kentucky Derby, and the Miss America pageant.

All the more reason, then, to know something about this particular region, its culture, its poetry, even if one has never ventured south of the Bunker Hill monument. Such books as Fred Hobson's *The Southern Writer in the Postmodern World* would appear to be helpful, but Hobson's writers are all novelists—poets are a breed apart, apparently.

Still, Hobson is useful: southern fiction is Thomas Wolfe and Flannery O'Connor and Walker Percy and (especially) William Faulkner, but it is also Josephine Humphreys and Fred Chappell, writers who continue that traditional strain emphasizing place, nature, family, and community, as well as Barry Hannah and Richard Ford, whose books provide a postmodern commentary on the traditional southern novel. In other words, Hobson's taxonomy describes the choices available to contemporary southern writers who can define themselves in ways forbidden to their ancestors.

Of course, writers have always tried to use their writing as a means of self-definition. Joseph Conrad, for example, made himself into an English novelist. Henry James, on the other hand, tried so hard to be one that he succeeded only in making obvious how irredeemably American he was, and the same is true for T. S. Eliot. Then there is Nabokov, floating between cultures and even disciplines like the lepidoptera he chased, but then that is a kind of self-defining, too.

For lyric poets, however, the issue of self-definition through writing is considerably more complex. An epic poet, a Homer or Dante or Milton, creates a work, a culture, and a self at one and the same time. But the lyric poet provides only glimpses of the self, and unless he or she is uncharacteristically programmatic, even one or more collections may be no more helpful as an aid to definition than a fistful of pieces would be in solving an entire picture puzzle. To use musical terms, if a novel is an opera, with visible characters moving through finite time and space, most poetry collections consist of the poet's Greatest Hits.

In his introduction to *Best American Poems 1991*, Mark Strand puts his finger on the special nature of poetry. "The context of a poem is likely to be only the poet's voice," he writes, "a voice speaking to no one in particular and unsupported by a situation or situations brought about by the words or actions of others, as in a work of fiction." The "work of fiction" Strand speaks of is clearly the Victorian behemoth: dense in detail, rich in event, obedient to the laws of Newtonian physics. And his "poem" is the lyric, Wordsworth's ruminations on a solitary reaper or Dickinson's address to a bee:

> A novel, if it is to be believed, must share characteristics with the world we live in. Its people must act in ways we recognize as human, and do so in places and with objects that seem believable. We are better prepared for reading fiction because most of what it tells us is already known. In a poem, most of what is said is neither known nor unknown. The world of things or the world of experience that may have given rise to the poem usually fades into the background. It is as if the poem were replacing that world as a way of establishing its own primacy, oddly asserting itself over the world.

So far as it goes, Strand's distinction between novel and poem is accurate, based as it is on the way the genres relate differently to the world, the one replacing it through point-by-point duplication, the other through transcendence. So if we are to define southern poetry, we will have to look at it as an original species and not as a cousin or other blood relation of southern fiction.

2. "VITAL RELATIONSHIPS"

The poets I have examined for the purpose of defining a southern poetry represent a fairly comprehensive range of genders, generations, and ethnicities. One thing most of them have in common, explicitly or implicitly, is an understanding of the contemporary world in terms of that cultural paradigm shift known as postmodernism and specifically the blurring of boundaries and polarities as everything becomes more and more like everything else. In the 1940s and '50s, Jean-Paul Sartre and Simone Weil warned against a growing monotony, a repetitiveness and sameness described by Jean Baudrillard, Frederic Jameson, Jean-François Lyotard, and others and often invoked by the term *simulacrum* or "copy." To this way of thinking, life imitates itself instead of advancing: Asian farmers dream of Levis and Coca-Cola, Europe becomes a theme park amidst the pines and scrub oaks of central Florida, and McDonald's continues its kudzu-like crawl from continent to continent.

Against all this self-duplication, poetry works as a momentary stay. Driving on I-95 in Florida, A. R. Ammons passes a Dantesque ziggurat of steaming refuse and thinks: "garbage has to be the poem of our time because / garbage is spiritual, believable enough // to get our attention, getting in the way, piling / up, stinking, turning brooks brownish and // creamy white: what else deflects us from the errors of our illusionary ways."

Out at Ammons's landfill, poetry succeeds in defeating the world's sameness first by paralleling it:

> The heap of knickknacks (knickknackatery),
> whatnots (whatnotery), doodads, jew's-harps,
>
> belt buckles, do-funnies, files, disks, pads,
> pesticide residues, nonprosodic high-tension
>
> lines, whimpering-wimp dolls, epichlorohydrin
> elastomotors, sulfur dioxide emissions, perfume
>
> sprays, radioactive williwaws: the people at
> Marine Shale are said to be "able to turn
>
> wastes into safe products": but some say these
> "products are themselves hazardous wastes":
>
> well, what does anybody want: is there a world
> with no bitter aftertaste or post coital triste:

and then tunneling under it, because

poetry is itself like an installation at Marine

Shale: it reaches down into the dead pit
and cool oil of stale recognition and words and

brings up hauls of stringy gook which it arrays
with light and strings with shiny syllables and

gets the mind back into vital relationships with
communication channels: but, of course, there

is some untransformed material, namely the poem
itself.

Under the world of sameness, then, poetry discovers what remains different. It does not communicate everything it finds, which is more the job of fiction. That is one more distinguishing characteristic of poetry, that it is less subject than fiction to a demand for clarity. As Ammons says, "poems / that give up the ideal of making sense do not // give up the ideal of not making sense."

In addition to saying that not making sense is a poetic ideal, Ammons might also observe that the words of poetry often remind us that much is communicated using media other than words. Hats, for example: a poem by Earl S. Braggs entitled simply "Hats" begins with an epigraph by Booker T. Washington: "Hats play an important part in the emotions of men. . . . The first thing the freed slaves thought about was a name and the second was a hat." The title poem makes it clear that hats are connected not only with identity but life itself; here George Jackson, the activist/prisoner who was killed during an escape attempt from San Quentin in 1971, says,

I have, like most people, a recurring dream
of being alive, tilting my hat to the blue side
of the dancing room and sliding a James Brown . . .

Not every poem in Braggs's collection is about hats, but quality headgear stands for the small things that are indispensable, the simple, nonverbal, everyday items that are *us*. It could be a hat; as the title of one poem says, it could be "Redbeans, Rice, and a Good Radio Station." In a world bent on photocopying itself and then copying the copies, it is through down-home objects such as these that we tell ourselves who we are.

Yet there is nothing in any of these books that embraces smugness, self-satisfaction; there is no poetic equivalent of the bumper sticker that says, "If your [picture of a heart] ain't in Dixie, get your [picture of a donkey] out!" More than one reader will identify with Elizabeth Seydel Morgan's image of the bookworm in the tree house, half in love with the summer's easeful heat and half ready to swap her perch in that pink mimosa for any other place in the world:

> But lazy didn't matter then
> as long as I could read and leave Atlanta,
> uncurling like a newborn from the cramp
> of time and space I was a child in,
> the embarrassment of hours inside the house.

Many of Morgan's poems argue that what seems essentially southern goes by other names elsewhere and vice versa; her "Daphne's Blues," for example, begins with Ovid's description of the goddess "in wild disarray" and Apollo thinking that she would look better dressed up and coiffed:

> Didn't you hear him Daddy
> Hear him say
> Didn't you hear him Daddy
> What he'd say—
>
> She's a fine lookin woman
> but she'd look finer *my* way.

Passion, possessiveness, perms: some things never change, from the groves of prehistory to some tin-roofed juke joint on the truck route. In *The Governor of Desire,* southern folkways are comforting because they are familiar, not superior. Far from it: a blues guitar echoes a shepherd's flute sounded long ago, and the hearer, in A. R. Ammons's garbage-ugly (though, I think, deliberately mock-bureaucratic) phrase, forgets the copycat world for a moment and "gets [her] mind back into vital relationships with communication channels."

3. "A SENSE OF FLIGHT"

The most lucid and engaging of the postmodern southern poets is John Wood, whose collection *In Primary Light* repeatedly iterates the "vital relationships" between the homely, even the grotesque, and the transcendent. A poem with a not-atypical title, "Upon Reading in the Newspaper That a Man in Kentucky Had Cut Off His Hand and His Foot with Pocketknives and Then Gouged Out an Eye in Order That He Might Go to Heaven," describes, well, pretty much that. Only when this God-fearing self-mutilator feels his life ebbing away, "having watched his arm and leg / gush like the garden hose he daily watered / his pole beans and collards with," he feels "his shoulder blades begin to grow / and push from his flesh and push with a softness, / a sweetness, a sense of flight." The poem begins in a uniquely American charnel house, a home surgery as revolting as Jeffrey Dahmer's kitchen or John Wayne Gacy's basement, and ends in Tuscany with the angels of Filippo Lippi and Fra Angelico.

Other Wood poems also confirm the links between low and high, pop and elite, southern and celestial. If his speakers make this admission grudgingly at first, they do so joyfully as the poems progress. Here, for example, are the first and last stanzas of "The Correct Answers":

We are all alike.

Everyone is alike

Everyone

is always alike:

hope, the bitch slut of history,

repeats the heart,

and we all live out

the old Magi journey.

. . . .

It's Christmas Eve

and I am in Arkansas

and will sit down tonight with family and eat;

and perhaps they will pray,

and then I will sleep.

And possibly

when I wake,

something will have happened,

will have descended

like gold or thighs

or even God, and I will·be

lifted, lifted

like flaming judgments from hope:

joyed and graced,

calm as the eyes

of a Sienese saint.

In another poem, Buddy Ebsen, patriarch of the archetypically southern Clampitt family on television, dies and goes to heaven and dances with Jesus, then God. In another, the speaker worries about the day in Mayberry when Opie stole apples "and Aunt Bea cried and cried / because she knew / he'd be at himself in a few years and that socks and sheets / would show his shame . . . / and that pimples would rise / on his face and that he would find his hands in sweaters / and his tongue deep into the cleft of the world's imperfections," because the South is just as edenic as the Garden ever was, and therefore Opie is as doomed to onanism (and worse) as Adam was to the old nine-to-five. A woman who passes out tracts appears in "The Canticle of End-Times," and in her thankless yet essential work of spreading the word about what is really real and what is not, she seems suspiciously like a poet.

Part of Wood's allure is that he is more "out" than the other postmodern southern poets, whose southernness, though unmistakable, tends to be embedded in a more cosmopolitan worldview. Another way of saying that would be to observe that, in preparing for this essay, at times I found myself reading only southern books and at others reading only the southern parts of books. But what is interesting in several of these collections in which there are comparatively few poems about southern themes or settings is how often the people in them are taken by surprise by their southernness, overwhelmed when they least expect it.

Take, for example, Charlie Smith's "The Dogwood Tree":

> your car broke down in rural Tennessee,
> and you walked along the road toward you hoped a town,
> and the road sank down onto its knees beside a stream,
> and the oaks hovered darkly in the air,
> the way the blossoms of a solitary dogwood tree
> that hung above the scattered grass,
> the freshened white disorder, colloquial as spit,
> walked straight into your body,
> and cleared you out of everything.

(Earlier the persona says of these same trees, "It's emptiness they want.")

The invasion is even more direct in Susan Ludvigson's "The Owl Snake" and, a page later, in "Blackberries," the one ending up in the speaker's lap, the other in her fist, her mouth, her dreams. Yet in the next poem, "October in the Aude," the speaker is again invaded by the natural world, only this time in France. Oddly, a true melding occurs here, in Europe. The speaker seems to feel more at home away from home as "sun spills / into my eyes, a blinding that makes pines / disappear in a golden blaze"; she floats "on the quick heat that could be / midsummer" as hawks circle overhead and there is, at least temporarily, a oneness between humankind and the rest of nature.

4. BRICOLAGE

A Freudian might say that these well-traveled southerners are being overwhelmed by an essential psychic component they thought they had successfully repressed. That would be a dated reading, though, because besides endless self-duplication, the other basic assumption of postmodernism is that, in a world where information moves more cheaply and rapidly with every passing second, everyone will participate more fluidly in a variety of once-opposed experiences: eating lunch at Burger King and dinner at Le Cirque, playing Goofy Golf in the afternoon and watching *Tannhäuser* at night, crawling with the owl snakes in the southern United States and soaring with the hawks in northern France.

In most of these collections, the South co-exists with other parts of the world. The most flamboyant example is Richard Katrovas's *The Book of Complaints*, which is divided into three parts: the first is devoted to contemporary Czechoslovakia, the second to prehistoric Greece, and the third to the South, especially New Orleans. Similarly, if less dramatically, Katherine Soniat's *A Shared Life* is full of cows and kudzu, but it also contains a poem called "A Square in Mozambique." Yet what affirms the indispensability of the South in all of these books is its presence as a common element: some deal with France, some with Czechoslovakia, and others with Mozambique, but they all deal with the South. It may not be too much to say that the South functions in the thought and art of these poets the same way it does in the culture at large. That is, the South is the smaller portion that gives the greater its vitality and focus. Postmodern southern poets define themselves, not southernly, but postmodernly; that is, they use the South as a key element in self-definition but not the only element.

Perhaps understandably, at least one of these poets is a little tentative about all this culture-juggling. In one of her poems, Alane Rollings asks, "am I just a re-assembler?" Memory being what it is, obviously the answer is some kind of qualified affirmative; in an essay entitled "The State of Southern Literary Scholarship," Lewis P. Simpson notes that an earlier southern author might have heard about the Battle of Gettysburg from his uncle, whereas a later one might have listened to an uncle as he recalled what *his* uncle told him (*Southern Review*, spring 1988). Yet as memories become less distinct as history, they become more distinct as art: even Rollings abandons her hesitancy about the artistic process to say, at one point, that

> You may be given only forty years more
> in which to say "brother" and "husband"
> with love created not so much of words, expressions on faces,
>   embraces
> as of your recollections of them: images that catch the light
> and move immaculately into view.

Other poets are more consistently assertive about their roles as *bricoleurs,* to use a term popular among postmodern theorists and sometimes translated not quite accurately as "handymen." The verb *bricoler* actually means to tinker or putter about, with the implication of assembling disparate objects (Ammons's "doodads" and "do-funnies"), often simply for one's own pleasure. Some, like Katherine Soniat, dramatize their *bricolage*: one of her speakers uses a blank page in a Gideon Bible to write a poem that describes, among other minglings, a herd of cows and buffaloes as well as signs that broadcast both troglodyte politics and the anti-abuse hotline number. Others, like Charlie Smith, comment more directly, as in a poem that begins "I'm looking everywhere for new ways, / poking, selecting, looking everywhere" and, in a vindication of the postmodernist way, ends "I'm tenderly / toasting the bread, I'm placing the saucer, / the spoon on the tray, I'm arranging the rose, / I'm pulling the curtain, I'm letting light flood the room."

Yet no poet is more confident of his handling of disparate materials than Wendell Berry. Ammons and he are the oldest in this group, and if Ammons represents the antic aspect of the aging seer, Berry represents his irascible side. In his sunnier moods, as suggested by poems like "A Third Possibility" and "Two Questions," Berry seems to be saying, "Enjoy everything—notice it all." But in more typical poems—in "The Record," for example, and "The Parting" and "One of Us"—Berry equates preserving and recording with pillaging. Enjoy it and let it go, he advises, saving his worst scorn for a videotaper who, in "The Vacation," films his leisure time instead of enjoying it, so that, ever after, "it would be there. With a flick / of a switch, there it would be. But he / would not be in it. He would never be in it." After a number of poems of the same tenor, a reader might be justified in thinking that the protagonist of "The Mad Farmer, Flying the Flag of Rough Branch, Secedes from the Union" is a version of Berry himself. The Mad Farmer does not want to live in a photocopied, videotaped world. The Mad Farmer wants to plunge up to his elbows in a real world, not a simulacrum.

At several points I have suggested that writers use brief, trenchant references to the South to energize larger worldviews. If that is the case, then perhaps the least southern of these poets is, in some ways, the most. Via *Radio Free Queens*, Virginia-born Susan Montez broadcasts stirring patriotic messages to those in exile, not from the South, but from the New York borough. Yet her affection for place rivals that of Faulkner, and her detailed depictions of Queens give it the status (on a smaller scale, of course) of Yoknapatawpha County. Indeed, one wonders if the poet is strapping her mask on just a little too tightly—is her hard-fought New York citizenship a telltale sign of her southernness, just as the ersatz Englishness of James and Eliot only reminds everyone of how American they are? This may be something of a stretch, but then readers too are *bricoleurs.*

If Montez emphasizes the essential southern love of place more than her peers, she emphasizes as well what Joel Williamson, in *William Faulkner and Southern History,* identifies as another quality essential to southern culture, namely, "placeness," an ungainly term that stands for the idea of there being a place for everyone in society, which he or she departs from (or tries to lure others from) at his or her own peril. Not surprisingly, Montez invokes that arch-taxonomist Dante Alighieri on the first page of her book. But then Charlie Smith alludes to Dante, and A. R. Ammons does, too.

5. HUMMINGBIRDS AND HICKORY STICKS

Come to think of it, what better household god to preside over the writing of postmodern southern poetry? Dante was a poet of both place and placeness, after all. Yet the place he created does not exist, and the placeness that gives shape to his hell amounts to little more than a settling of intensely private scores.

Mainly, though, Dante was a Florentine. He knew the whole world because he knew even better a tiny plot in northern Italy, just as, as different as they were from one another, Jefferson knew his world from the standpoint of Monticello and Goethe his from that of Weimar. And as different as they are, what each of these postmodern southern poets reminds us is that we need to walk before we can run, to eat chitlins before we try the foie gras, and to determine exactly where home is before we venture out into the world. Moving with a hummingbird speed possible only in lyric poetry, these poets advance and retreat along the taut, supple wire of their own voices.

Meanwhile, high in his Manhattan office, the op-ed columnist for the *Times* wakes from his fitful dreams of crazed rednecks and rattlesnake-handling Pentecostals to bludgeon a Boston hotel with the stick of southern hickory. And that, these postmodern southern poets may well say, is the point: if others think and write about us without cease, should we not think and write about ourselves?

The Poet as Pitchman

JAMES DICKEY, AMERICAN POET

Mention James Dickey to most people and they'll say, "Didn't he write *Deliverance?*" Yes, and he even appears in the 1972 movie version as the archetypal Southern sheriff who tells the city boys to get the hell out and stay out, too.

To others, Dickey was the Dylan Thomas of the South, the hard-living carouser whose poetry was deeply rooted in the soil, the boozy celebrity who was a larger-than-life (if occasionally embarrassing) advertisement for his native region. Touring relentlessly and appearing everywhere, he brought poetry to people who had never heard it before; to many, James Dickey is the last, and perhaps the only, poet they have read.

Athlete, outdoorsman, expert archer, and military vet, Dickey staked out the position of premier tough-guy writer that Hemingway held in the previous generation. In a 1990 interview, Dickey admitted that he had an "assumed personality" like Hemingway's, a "big, strong, hard drinking, hard fighting" public persona that hid the "timid, cowardly" Dickey, the aesthete who was also at home with authors like Oscar Wilde.

Oscar Wilde? Yes, for "there is something about the excessive that appeals to people. . . . As Oscar Wilde, a favorite of mine, says, nothing succeeds like excess."

Excess is the key to Dickey's life and work. Few writers have been praised and castigated in equal measure as Dickey has, and almost every time it has been his excesses that occasioned the laurels as well as the darts.

Born in Atlanta in 1923, Dickey was a football and track star in college (he attended Clemson briefly but graduated from Vanderbilt) and a fighter pilot in World War II and the Korean War. He had a successful career in advertising, writing copy for Coca-Cola, among others, though when his boss once said in a meeting, "Dickey writes poetry as a hobby," the poet claims he slammed his hand down on the table and roared, "Advertising is the hobby!"

Dickey wrote his first book, *Into the Stone* (1960), on company time. Shortly after, he left advertising to teach at a half-dozen universities before becoming poet-in-residence at the University of South Carolina in 1969. His writings include criticism, screenplays, children's books, and, of course, *Deliverance* (1970) as well as two other novels, *Alnilam* (1987) and *To the White Sea* (1993). The 1965 collection *Buckdancer's Choice* won the National Book Award for poetry.

And it will be largely for his poetry that Dickey will be remembered in years to come. His early poems, such as "The Performance," are often technically simple yet tightly organized presentations of primal scenes. In this stunning and moving poem, an acrobatic POW puts on a show of somersaults and handstands for his Japanese captors just before they cut off his head.

But the poems in *Buckdancer's Choice* and after are deliberately less finished, intentionally more dependent on the reader's involvement. Sparse punctuation, startling line breaks, and asymmetrical stanzas characterize poems like "The Shark's Parlor" and "Diabetes."

For all their differences, each of these poems is bold in subject matter, extravagant in diction—excessive, in a word. As are Dickey's three novels: the idea for *Deliverance* came to Dickey when he was living in Dante's Italy, and in fact the journey of the four Atlanta businessmen involves a descent to and return from a kind of inferno, complete with devils and grotesques.

Deliverance was followed in 1987 by *Alnilam*, a combination adventure story and semi-mystical treatise on flight. The story involves a secret group of Air Force pilots who worship one of their
number who may or may not have perished in a crash, but many
readers were overwhelmed by the sheer bulk of this 680-pager. If
there is any truth to hearsay, *Alnilam* was more often begun than
finished.

His final novel was *To the White Sea*, which, like the others—and
like the most memorable poetry, too—treats violence as though it
were instructive and, in that way, even attractive. *To the White Sea*
is the story of Muldrow, a downed tailgunner making his way across
war-torn Japan, killing ruthlessly as he seeks and finds obliteration
in the country's snowy north.

What links all of Dickey's writing is his predilection for outra-
geous imagery: a headless corpse on a beach, a man being raped
in the Georgia woods. In his 1990 interview, Dickey derides the
simplicity of Romantic poet William Blake, noting that "one gets
a little tired of Blake seeing heaven in a wild flower and eternity
in a grain of sand."

He is equally harsh with his contemporaries, chiding Adrienne
Rich for writing about a cockroach and Robert Lowell for focusing
on his own life. Among the classic American authors, he prefers
Emerson to Thoreau because Emerson is "a presenter of possibili-
ties," whereas Thoreau is "too much of a doctrine giver"; besides,
Emerson "opens up more territory than Thoreau."

By definition, though, excess means going too far, and any writer
who compares himself with Hemingway is cruising for a critical bruising. One critic titled his study *James Dickey: The Poet
as Pitchman* (though the poet himself preferred to describe his
self-promoting efforts as "barnstorming"), and another chides the
writer for "big-chested aphorisms," "an irritating portentousness,"
and "a pseudomythological strain," concluding that "Dickey, in
short, often gets in his own way, which may be the wage he pays
for his reputedly big ego."

Big images, big ego: Dickey was an easy target for those who think he went too far. Yet even his detractors admit that he is one of the finest poets of the sixties, and it is not uncommon to find a largely negative review ending with a sentence like "even his failures are ambitious, and in a handful of poems he has given us something to remember."

From start to finish, Dickey's poetry is wrenchingly visceral. One of his last poems to appear in print is "Last Hours," a letter of sorts to a dying brother that is organized partly around a startling book, a biography of serial killer Ted Bundy the dying man's daughter is reading to him to distract him from the approach of his own death. "Follow / The murderer," says the poem, in what must be one of the strangest admonitions ever to a dying man, "for he has caught the interest / of your brain's last blood."

But there is nothing mild about poetry to the Dickey who once said, "What you have to realize when you write poetry, or if you love poetry, is that poetry is just naturally the greatest goddamn thing that ever was in the whole universe." Poetry was central to the life of Dickey the writer, and Dickey the barnstormer made poetry central to the lives of countless others.

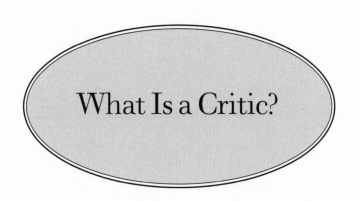

What Is a Critic?

Emerson, Poe, and American Criticism in the Nineteenth Century

The fundamental difference between early and later American literary criticism is easy to discern—it's that the early criticism is more intimately connected to national life. There was, in early America, nothing equivalent to the present complex and interlocking system of universities, academic presses, scholarly journals, literary conferences, and so on. Thus early literary criticism was conducted outside of a professional (some might say professorial) context. Whereas twentieth-century criticism takes place largely within a university environment and is shaped by both the privileges and the penalties born of a certain objective remove, early criticism is closely involved with the actual historical development of the nation itself and, in many ways, actually mirrors that development.

The rigors of colonial life did not encourage belles lettres—hard to write a couplet when you're trying to build a stockade—and thus the earliest works are autobiographical in nature. Puritan authors such as John Winthrop and William Bradford favored such genres as the diary, the essay, the letter, and the sermon, works that emphasize survival and salvation rather than artistic elegance. Franklin, Paine, Jefferson, and the other great authors of the revolutionary generation focused on politics and philosophy—again, work destined to be read for other than aesthetic reasons.

The generation of Irving and Cooper, while still writing with an

English readership in mind, began to lay claim slowly to American subjects and modes of expression, and a corresponding critical tradition began to form. In the years between 1810 and 1835, there were more than 130 magazines that might be considered literary. But in the absence of a robust literary context, the majority of the reviews and articles were written by lawyers, lawmakers, ministers, physicians, and schoolmasters rather than poets and novelists. The resultant criticism has a judicial and moral flavor that makes most of it forgettable.

It was not until the 1840s, which heralded the explosive appearance of dozens of now-classic works by American romantics and realists, that a mature criticism began to appear as an accompaniment to the literature itself. Emerson and Poe were the most important critics of the midcentury, with the one articulating a theory of literature that looks at its nature, function, and purpose and the other concerning himself with theory as well but also with poetics or questions of craft.

During that remarkable period known as the American Renaissance, several key developments occurred simultaneously: (1) the first generation of professional writers appeared; (2) many of the enduring works of American literature appeared as well; and (3) a criticism appeared that focused on American writing as an independent type rather than a British derivative. This native literary criticism ranges from extremes that are highly idealistic at one pole and almost scientifically practical at the other, thus laying the groundwork for a broad spectrum of criticism to come. Perhaps not surprisingly, the authors of *The Scarlet Letter, Moby-Dick, Leaves of Grass,* and *Daisy Miller* also wrote much of the most enduring criticism of the period.

The first radical call to arms for writers comes from Emerson, whose essay "The Poet" (1844) is a classic of romantic literary theory. Breaking with neoclassical thought, in which formalism curbs fluid expression, Emerson calls not for meters but for a meter-making argument in poetry, and a precedence of thought over form. He seeks a specifically American poet, one who will not only rival but even exceed Homer and Shakespeare. Admitting that he sees no such poet yet in America, Emerson maintains nonetheless that the next great poet will create his work in New World groves and pastures rather than in the castles of Europe. He also emphasizes the importance of poetry to society as a liberating force, one that opens the eyes of its readers to new views. In this seminal essay, Emerson also creates a foundation for the type of criticism called theory, which is devoted to the broader purposes of literature, as opposed to poetics, which deals with the mechanics of its composition.

In sharp contrast to Emerson's theoretical criticism, Poe offers a distinctly practical view of poem-making in "The Philosophy of Composition" (1846). Rejecting the romantic assumption that the writer is an instrument responding instinctively to stimuli beyond his ken, Poe argues that it is possible and even desirable for a literary work to be constructed with the rigor and precision of a mathematical problem. Taking "The Raven" as his example, Poe describes his search for the perfect length (one hundred lines, though the finished poem turns out to be one hundred and eight), province (Beauty), tone (sadness), and artistic effect (the refrain, which, because of its monotony, would be spoken most logically by a nonhuman creature). The point of a raven saying "Nevermore" at the end of each stanza of a melancholy poem of roughly one hundred lines is to dramatize what Poe calls the most poetical topic in the world, namely, the death of a beautiful woman, and to present that topic from the point of view of the perfect narrator, the bereaved lover who is tormented by grief as well as the utterances of the infernal bird. Here Poe espouses a poetics of literature, which, unlike theory, is concerned with craft rather than function.

Emerson and Poe represent the extremes of early American literary criticism, the first positioning art within the broader spectrum of all human endeavor and the latter examining closely a set of finite precepts. As the Industrial Revolution progressed and new technologies made publication easier for an increasingly literate readership, new outlets for literary expression appeared along with new voices, both literary and critical, and it was not long before criticism became as diverse as literature itself. The genteel, schoolmasterly approach that appealed to the general reader is represented by James Russell Lowell's "Fable for Critics" (1848), with its witty estimates of such contemporaries as Longfellow, Holmes, Bryant, and Whittier. But there was also biographical criticism, as evidenced in Rufus Griswold's scandal-mongering obituary of Poe and an edition of Poe's letters (1850) to which he added passages favorable to himself.

Margaret Fuller's *Woman in the Nineteenth Century* (1845) is the first mature consideration of feminism in American life. Her essay "American Literature: Its Position in the Present Time, and Prospects for the Future" (1846) laments the lack of an American literature per se but proposes a list of worthy contemporaries, concluding that "the future is glorious . . . for those who do their duty in the present." Magazines such as *Godey's Lady's Book* (1830–98) influenced fashion, manners, and literary taste thanks to editors such as Sarah J. Hale, who, in her forty years with the monthly, published not only Emerson and Poe but Harriet Beecher Stowe as well. Frederick Douglass's *Narrative of the Life of Frederick Douglass* (1845) and his later autobiographies as well as Harriet Jacobs's *Incidents in the Life of a Slave Girl* (1861), with its authorial preface and supportive testimonials by Jacobs's defenders, argue the case for minority viewpoints as a significant aspect of American literary expression. The 1850s also saw the publication of the first novel by a Native American, the Cherokee John Rollin Ridge's *Life and Adventures of Joaquín Murieta* (1854).

In all of its variety, nineteenth-century literary criticism continued to position itself between Emerson's theory and Poe's poetics. Melville, for example, champions American writers almost as loudly as Emerson does, yet his rhetoric is more grounded in the realities of American life. Too, unlike Emerson, Melville has found his ideal native writer, as the title of his essay "Hawthorne and His Mosses" (1851) suggests. Melville likens his new hero to an old one, saying that Hawthorne and Shakespeare share a sense of mirth but an even greater sense of tragedy and that the American novelist's work, moreover, is characterized by subtleties as fine as any in Shakespeare. Melville insists that present-day Shakespeares are being born this very day on the banks of the Ohio. What is needed, he claims, is a more professional corps of reviewers to assess American genius. Melville is clearly thinking of the generally sorry state of magazine criticism in the early republic as well as the pointedly unkind reception of some of his own writing when he notes that "there are hardly five critics in America; and several of them are asleep"!

Melville's judgment is harsh but perhaps not entirely undeserved, considering the failure of nineteenth-century literary journalists to comprehend the subtleties of much of his own work. The critical writing with the greatest impact continued to come from the literary artists themselves, often in the form of comment on their own work. In his preface to *The House of the Seven Gables* (1851), Hawthorne draws a careful distinction between the novel, with its professed goal of describing faithfully the actual world, and a form much more congenial to himself and other early American writers, the romance. Hawthorne's entire literary output is shot through with the ecstasy as well as the anxiety of the author who is trying to free himself of the confines of Old World fiction and put a new kind in its place. Accordingly, in his preface he claims a certain authorial latitude toward the reality he wishes to depict. Whereas the novel limits itself to the probable and the ordinary, the romance may concern itself with the possible. Both genres must deal with truth, but the romancer has more freedom as to the circumstances under which truth will be presented and thus, as Hawthorne says,

can raise or lower the lights or deepen and enrich the shadows in
his fictional picture. Hawthorne cautions a moderate use of these
authorial privileges and urges the romancer not to season the dish
he offers the public with too much of the marvelous, though he
suggests that to disregard this advice would not be a literary crime.

If Hawthorne is closer here to the poetics of Poe, then Whitman,
like Melville before him, is closer to the theoretical approach of
Emerson. This hardly is surprising, for even though Whitman was
one of the most radical technical innovators of any literary period
he was also a steward of the transcendental tradition, which argued
for the preeminence of the individual over the authority of institutions. Indeed, Whitman was the ideal poet that Emerson called for
in his own essay, and when he sent the Sage of Concord a copy of the
1855 edition of *Leaves of Grass,* the older writer replied, "I greet
you at the beginning of a new career" (in a letter that Whitman
reprinted in future editions, to Emerson's considerable annoyance).

In his preface to the 1855 edition, Whitman asserts his belief that
the United States themselves are their own greatest poem, a nation
among nations that is, at the same time, a literary text with as many
spaces, as many opposites and contradictions as the soul requires to
find its own homelike niche. In a catalog of the sort that typifies
"Song of Myself" and other poems, Whitman praises American
speech, dress, friendship, love of freedom, curiosity, delight in music, evenness of temper, even Americans' quickness to anger as well
as their shambling walk. Yet unlike Emerson, Whitman doesn't
rebel against European ideas but rather embraces and combines
them with American ones. Whitman's celebrated "catalogs"—here
of geographical features, species of birds, professions—culminate
in a paean to political liberty and the poet's eagerness to know all
and embrace all, including venereal sores, masturbation, the burst
capillaries of alcoholics, the vileness of seducers and prostitutes and
sexual perverts. If Whitman's belief that priests will disappear and
poets take their place seems like wishful thinking, or that a poet's

country will absorb him as affectionately as he absorbs it, is, in his own case, clearly doomed, at least he sets the stage for writers of generations to come and substantiates their freedom of choice as to technique and subject matter.

Henry James, who was to become the first of the truly modern American literary critics, began his career as a student of the famous writers who preceded him, though he distanced himself from both an optimism about American writing that at times bordered on the jingoistic as well as a critical impressionism that often ignored the writer's craft. The most prolific of the authors mentioned thus far, James published, in addition to his many works of fiction, numerous reviews and critical essays, including the book-length *Hawthorne* (1879). Here James echoes both Hawthorne's own regret over the historical thinness of American life as well as his realization that this deficiency can be a goad to the imaginative powers of American writers and readers alike. If America lacks a sovereign, an aristocracy, a centuries-old church, an even older artistic culture, and a venerable political and military along with the palaces and castles that keep history alive in present-day minds, then the novelist lacks the ready-made advantage of the English writer, who is presented with a preexisting world at birth and needs simply add his own touches to it. By contrast, the American writer must paint his entire novelistic world from the ground up, which, to James, explains the prevalence of whimsy in American writing. The American reader, too, must rely more on his instincts than his English counterpart.

It is essential that the reader read between the lines, complete the writer's suggestions, and aid the writer in constructing his picture. By bringing the reader into the picture and making him an active participant in the writing process, James turned away from the belief shared by critics as different as Emerson and Poe that the writer is a larger-than-life puppet master who controls the reader's responses. William Dean Howells, himself a novelist and James's friend and editor as well, also champions readerly independence in *Criticism and Fiction* (1891), one chapter of which is entitled "Realism and the Common Man."

James's best-known essay is "The Art of Fiction" (1884), initially a response to a lecture by the Victorian novelist Sir Walter Besant. Whereas Besant maintained that fiction was a fine art like painting or music and should be studied in terms of the immutable laws that governed it, James puts much more emphasis on the novelist's powers of imagination, arguing that the writer's job is to pull the unseen out of the seen. The novel is a free and elastic form governed as much by the writer's and reader's depth of mind as by the outside world. A novel has no moral purpose, as claimed by Besant and such American critics as William Crary Brownell, and instead must offer a sense of deeply felt life. Recall James's famous advice to aspiring novelists in "The Art of Fiction": "Try to be one of the people on whom nothing is lost!" Taking issue with the aristocratic Besant's insistence that a novelist must know his or her place, James argues that to possess a first-rate mind permits a young woman who lives in a quiet village to write of military life and a blue-collar novelist to write of high society.

Between 1905 and 1909, James wrote the eighteen prefaces to the so-called New York Edition of his collected fiction. In these essays he counters the impressionistic criticism of the day with a craftsman's rigor, contributing ideas and technical terms still used by literary critics today. Among other topics, he discusses the portrayal of time in fiction; the creation of place; the use of indirection and ambiguity; the importance of using dramatic techniques in fiction; and, perhaps most important, the merit of the "center of consciousness" technique in such novels as *The Portrait of a Lady* (1882).

In James's late criticism, with its emphasis on formalism, American literary criticism made a marked advance toward professionalism. Not an academic himself, James set the stage for the academic critical industry that would grow steadily after World War I and then explosively in the midcentury and beyond. If nineteenth-century criticism sometimes seems almost overwhelmingly approving of both American life and literature, twentieth-century criticism often seems the opposite as it interrogates, resists, and, in its most extreme forms, attacks not only American culture in general but also its specifically literary artifacts.

As a profession that can, like the creation of literature itself, now be pursued full-time, contemporary American literary criticism is constantly evolving. At the same time, there is no new thing under the sun, as Ecclesiastes says—critics are still working the field that Emerson and Poe laid out for them, with theory at the one end and poetics at the other.

Slouching toward Baltimore

TWENTIETH-CENTURY LITERARY CRITICISM

Just past the turn of the century, the gulf seems wider than ever between two critical camps. The first consists of a dominant minority of cutting-edge academics who practice a rigorous, occasionally esoteric, often politicized, and undeniably jargonistic mix of critical approaches that developed largely in Europe and are referred to generally as "theory." The other camp consists of the academic majority, who are content to teach literature much as they were taught it by their own professors, offering an eclectic mix of biography, close reading, impressionism, and borrowings from critics with marquee names (including, of course, many theorists). Most students, literary journalists and reviewers, trade editors, and lay readers belong to this second group as well.

Thanks to its activism, the theory group gets most of the attention these days, with the result that, to observers both within and without the academy, the terms "criticism" and "theory" have become identical. But criticism has always consisted of both theory, which concerns itself with the function of literature, and poetics, which deals with craft. In ancient Greece, for example, Plato offers a theory of art in *The Republic* (360 B.C.), where philosophers rule as arbiters of truth and beauty and from which the less rational poets are exiled; Aristotle's *Poetics* (350 B.C.), on the other hand, deals with the necessary ingredients of a successful play. To take a more recent example, in mid-nineteenth-century America, Emerson's essay "The Poet" (1844) is a classic example of theory in its call for literary nationalism, whereas Poe offers a poetics in "The Philosophy of Composition" (1846), a kind of recipe for effective poem construction.

Twentieth-century critics continue to work this same venerable field, marked off by theory at one boundary and poetics at the other. Many of the most influential critics practice both types of criticism, as is the case with Henry James, the last great critic of the nineteenth century, the first great one of the twentieth, and the source of ideas and techniques that will continue to shape both fiction and criticism in the years to come; he was also the first truly international American critic, one as much at home with the works of Trollope, Flaubert, and Turgenev as those of Hawthorne. In the eighteen prefaces to the New York Edition of his collected fiction (1907–9), James approaches fiction with a craftsman's rigor in his discussions of time, place, narration, and other technical matters. Clearly, though, James's poetics grow out of his theory of the novel, described earliest in "The Art of Fiction" (1884) as an elastic form capable of conveying a sense of deeply felt life as long as both writer and reader bring great force of mind to bear on it. For most of the twentieth century, the most important criticism of the novel included both theory and poetics in varying proportion, with critics not only describing the nature and role of the novel but also suggesting—sometimes subtly, sometimes strongly—how the novelist should write.

In calling for a more formalistic attitude toward the novel, James was reacting against the late-Victorian moralism that often valued a work of fiction more for its piety than its aesthetics. Naturally, the next generation included critics disturbed by what they saw as too much formalism, an art-for-art's-sake standard unchecked by a proper concern with ethics. The so-called New Humanism, a conservative movement in American philosophy and literary criticism in the 1920s, was a reaction against naturalism and stressed

the moral qualities of literature; in turn, it would give way to the
New Criticism and to Marxist and Freudian approaches to literature. Prominent New Humanists include Irving Babbitt, whose
early work *The New Laokoön* (1910) called for classical restraint
in American writing and who later attacked Theodore Dreiser and
Sinclair Lewis for surrendering to modern chaos, and Paul Elmer
More, author of *The Demon of the Absolute* (1928) and other works,
who labeled John Dos Passos's *Manhattan Transfer* (1925) "an ex-
plosion in a cesspool."

Like any critics working from a conservative viewpoint, the New
Humanists failed to appreciate the experimental work of their day,
work that has since become part of the canon. This was left to such
critics as Edmund Wilson, a literary polymath who took a number of critical stances during his long career, never aligning himself closely with any one school. His first major book, *Axel's Castle*
(1931), treats modernism as a mating of naturalism and symbolism,
as seen in the writing of James Joyce, Marcel Proust, and Gertrude
Stein; a later volume, *The Shores of Light* (1952), studies the work
of F. Scott Fitzgerald and his contemporaries. A novelist himself,
Wilson responded to fiction on the aesthetic, psychological, and political levels, thus embodying the major trends of the next several
decades of literary criticism.

The most important aesthetic approach to literature in this
century is formalism, whether of the Russian kind or the Anglo-
American New Critical variety. Both Russian formalists and New
Critics emphasized detailed, logical examinations of a work's literary devices, but whereas the New Critics tended to distill their
findings into humanistic aphorisms, the Russian formalists focused
entirely on form, excluding the work's moral and cultural significance. As with every critical school, Russian formalism evolved
into different camps; the Bakhtinian school, so-called after Mikhail
Bakhtin, its most influential practitioner, viewed language as a social phenomenon. In his *Problems of Dostoevsky's Poetics* (1929),

Bakhtin observes that, whereas Tolstoy wrote a "monologic" type of novel in which the various voices are subordinated to the author's, Dostoevsky wrote a "polyphonic" or "dialogic" type in which the voices of different characters are not merged with or subordinated to the author's but maintain their own integrity.

The New Criticism is a method of close reading whose sources include the French tradition of *explication de texte*, the essays of T. S. Eliot, I. A. Richards's *The Principles of Literary Criticism* (1924), and William Empson's *Seven Types of Ambiguity* (1930). Facetiously yet with some accuracy called "the lemon-squeezing school" of literary criticism, the New Critics examine the text as an object in itself, excluding authorial biography and historical context and looking at the work's images, symbols, diction, and use of irony and other devices in its presentation of a single, complex, and well-wrought point. Influenced by Jules Laforgue and other French symbolists, Eliot and Ezra Pound were, in fact, writing a kind of poem that called for a new type of criticism; in the United States, John Crowe Ransom, Allen Tate, and other members of the so-called Fugitive group furthered the notion that a work of literature reflected neither the author's life nor grand moral themes but was instead an experience in itself.

As the New Criticism expanded, its focus shifted from the lyric poem to all genres, including the novel, just as the practice of it changed thanks to critics as different as R. P. Blackmur, who examined the European novel and those of Henry James in such works as *The Double Agent* (1935), and Yvor Winters, whose *Maule's Curse* (1938) looks at the writings of Hawthorne and Poe.

The two great popularizers of the New Criticism, Cleanth Brooks and Robert Penn Warren, first encountered each other as undergraduates at Vanderbilt, then as Rhodes scholars at Oxford, and then as faculty at Louisiana State University, where they founded the *Southern Review* and, as one observer noted, moved the center of literary criticism in the West "from the left bank of the

Seine to the left bank of the Mississippi." Both ended up at Yale,
Brooks continuing to produce important theoretical work and Warren extending the Jamesian tradition of composing both literature
and commentary on it. Their joint efforts include two widely used
textbooks, *Understanding Poetry* (1938) and *Understanding Fiction* (1943), and, though their work has been challenged by other
critical approaches, the New Criticism continues to be highly influential, because the close reading method not only serves as the
basis for many of the subsequent approaches but also, as an examination of best-selling textbooks shows, is the one still preferred by
the majority of classroom teachers.

In its purest form, the New Criticism prospered between the
1930s and 1950s, along with Freudian criticism, a sort of cousin
to it, as well as a wholly unrelated Marxist criticism. Joseph Wood
Krutch's *Edgar Allan Poe: A Study in Genius* (1926) is an early work
of the Freudian school that examines the artist's neuroses using
psychoanalytic techniques. In *The Triple Thinkers* (1938) and *The
Wound and the Bow* (1941), Edmund Wilson looks at James, Edith
Wharton, and Ernest Hemingway from a Freudian angle, emphasizing in the latter work the idea that the mature artist is com-
pensating for a trauma received earlier in life. Other influential
Freudian commentaries include Kenneth Burke's *The Philosophy
of Literary Form* (1941), which sees literature as an expression of
the writer's conflicts, and Leslie Fiedler's *Love and Death in the
American Novel* (1960). A novelist himself, Fiedler offers here the
provocative yet persuasive idea that the classic image in American
culture is of two men, one light-skinned and one dark, fleeing civilization (and women) and clinging to their ideal of boyish together-
ness, a paradigm that can be seen in the novels of James Fenimore
Cooper, Edgar Allan Poe, Mark Twain, Truman Capote, and Ken
Kesey as well as in today's "buddy movies." Frederick Crews used
Freudian methods in *Sins of the Fathers: Hawthorne's Psychological
Themes* (1966) but repudiated the Viennese master in *The Mem-*

ory Wars: Freud's Legacy in Dispute (1995). The Freud that Crews embraces and then spurns is a kind of mental mechanic familiar to American readers. In France, however, the criticism of Jacques Lacan and his followers adumbrates the vision of Freud the humanist, a more tentative, artistic thinker.

Just as the terms "New Critical" and "Freudian" changed in meaning as these movements spread, so, too, does "Marxist criticism" take on a variety of hues over time. A precursor of the Marxist approach can be found in Vernon Parrington's three-volume *Main Currents in American Thought* (1927–1930), a historical examination of progressive American ideas and their expression in literature. Granville Hicks's *The Great Tradition* (1933), on the other hand, is a forthright measurement of American literature since the Civil War according to the standards of orthodox Marxism. Predictably, Marxist attacks and counterattacks flourished heatedly in journal essays, from the crude fulminations of Mike Gold in *The New Masses* to the subtle offerings in Philip Rahv's *Partisan Review.* Edmund Wilson incorporated less-strident versions of Marxist views in his books and essays while pointing out that politics were no substitute for aesthetics, and critics as different as F. O. Matthiessen, Lionel Trilling, Irving Howe, Mary McCarthy, and Alfred Kazin, all of whom had at least one foot in the socialist or liberal camp, were flexible in blending sociopolitical commentary with humanistic literary judgments.

But "humanism," with its implications of classical order, rationalism, and morality, is a term that has largely disappeared from the vocabulary of the most visible critics of the last half of the twentieth century, namely, the practitioners of the various reading strategies called "theory." These strategies had their origin in the 1911 publication of Ferdinand de Saussure's *Course in General Linguistics.* Saussure argued that words are arbitrary, that "horse" has no innate connection with the animal to which it refers. Saussureans make this point by listing the radically different nouns used in various languages to describe the same creature: English "horse," for example, but German "Pferd" and French "cheval." Here are three words that do not come close to resembling each other, yet a three-year-old would know instantly what a speaker meant were he to use one, providing the speaker and the child were conversing in the same language. To a German child, then, "horse" and "cheval" would mean nothing, which is Saussure's larger point: words mean nothing.

In the absence of meaning, what particular groups of humans share is an agreement to recognize a common code of signifiers ("horse") that apply to the signifieds (an equine quadruped). This allows people to have conversations and read the newspaper, but all conversations and texts are coded. Thus there is no right or wrong language, no language better or worse for describing reality. Instead, all language is code and thus separate from reality. Therefore, one might say that language is the only reality or at least the only one that counts. If there is no objective external reality (how can there be if there are all those different languages?), then there is only half-conscious linguistic interplay between perceiver and perceived. We humans, our world: everything is made of language and language only. Everything is a text.

From Saussure's arcane linguistic assumptions comes one universal idea that can be applied to virtually any discipline, namely, that there is no self, that we and our institutions are inhabited by hidden, impersonal structures. The anthropologist Claude Lévi-Strauss was the first to apply Saussure's ideas outside of the field of linguistics. Structuralism, as Lévi-Strauss called his analytical method, assumed that tribal groups were governed by systems of relations of which they were unaware, unconscious but consistent laws that determined the tribe's actions.

And if that is true for the South American Indians whom Lévi-Strauss studied, then it must be true for other communities as well. From structuralism, then, to the present proliferation of theoretical strategies known collectively as poststructuralism, beginning with semiotics or the science of signs. Semioticians study not just tribes and texts but everything: Robert Scholes's *Semiotics and Interpretation* (1982) discusses not only poems, stories, and a scene from a play but also movies, bumper stickers, and, as he says delicately in his preface, "a portion of the human anatomy." This latter turns out to be the clitoris, which, as signifiers go, is uncommonly tricky. For one thing, its pronunciation is unsettled, with some dictionaries accenting the second syllable and others the first. The *OED* defines it as "a homologue of the male penis," thus defining the clitoris in terms of something other than itself, and so on.

In addition to the structuralists (Lévi-Strauss) and the semioticians (Barthes), the theory group also includes philosophically, psychoanalytically, and economically grounded thinkers: Heideggerians (Jacques Derrida), Nietzscheans (Michel Foucault), Freudians (Jacques Lacan), and Marxists (Lucien Goldmann). As different as these poststructuralist thinkers are, each is telling us that there is no us: that cultural structures or the media or corrupt Western thought or the will to power or the unconscious mind or bogus economic systems make us what we are. Or what we seem to be, since, in fact, we are not.

To the general reader, David Lodge's novel *Nice Work* (1988) offers a useful introduction to deconstruction, the most famous (or infamous) of the various poststructural strategies. Lodge's novel tells the story of an unlikely affair between two very different characters, the businessman Vic Wilcox and an *au courant* academic, Robyn Penrose. Robyn is so up-to-date that she believes the whole idea of character to be "a bourgeois myth, an illusion created to reinforce the ideology of capitalism." It is no accident that the idea of the literary character developed simultaneously with the rise of capitalism, since "both are expressions of a secularized Protestant ethic, both dependent on the idea of an autonomous individual self who is responsible for and in control of his/her own destiny, seeking happiness and fortune in competition with other autonomous selves." But Robyn knows that "there is no such thing as the 'self' on which capitalism and the classic novel are founded—that is to say, a finite, unique soul or essence that constitutes a person's identity; there is only a subject position in an infinite web of discourses—the discourses of power, sex, family, science, religion, poetry, etc."

These Derridean principles work well for Robyn Penrose in the academy, but they are put to the test when she meets Vic Wilcox and they begin their affair. Vic is intelligent if uninitiated; his problem is that he is an essentialist, one who believes each of us is an essence that exists independent of language, whereas Robyn believes in language alone. The lovers never do fully understand each other—or at least Vic never fully understands Robyn. When they are in bed together and he puts his hand between her legs, Robyn tells Vic that "the discourse of romantic love pretends that your finger and my clitoris are extensions of two unique individual selves who need each other and only each other and cannot be happy without each other for ever and ever." "That's right," says Vic. "I love your silk cunt with my whole self, for ever and ever." Fictional businessman Vic Wilcox is not as ambiguous about the female anatomy as real-life theorist Robert Scholes, and even Robyn Penrose is described as "not unmoved by this declaration."

But of course the affair is doomed, though not before author Lodge dramatizes some important ideas in a manner that is comical yet sympathetic to both old-fashioned thinking and newer approaches such as deconstruction. Or he would have had such a creature as "author Lodge" ever existed. In the earlier discussion of capitalism and its relation to the delusional concept of character (which, to a deconstructionist, does not exist), Lodge's narrator observes that, "by the same token, there is no such thing as an author" and that, instead, "every text is a product of intertextuality, a tissue of allusions to and citations of other texts; and, in the famous words of Jacques Derrida (famous to people like Robyn, anyway), *'il n'y a pas de hors-texte,'* there is nothing outside the text."

Derrida was one of a group of thinkers representing the various schools of theory who appeared at a 1966 Johns Hopkins University symposium called "The Language of Criticism and the Sciences of Man." This symposium was the historical event that, in the course of a few days, changed permanently the reading, teaching, and writing of literature in the United States. In that instance, the Hopkins campus became the Plymouth Rock for the arrival in America of "theory," most of whose founding fathers were there: Goldmann, Barthes, Lacan, Tzvetan Todorov, and, chiefly, Derrida, who gave a talk entitled "Structure, Sign, and Play in the Discourse of the Human Sciences."

His pronouncement that "there is nothing outside of the text" encapsulates one of deconstruction's most controversial doctrines. After all, how announce to an ambitious novelist or poet "The Death of the Author," to use the title of Roland Barthes's 1977 essay that serves as a lightning rod for so much anti-deconstructionist sentiment? How tell a writer, especially one who has already received recognition of some kind and is beginning to think of making a career of authorship, "You do not exist"? To answer that question requires a look at the Barthes essay as well as one by Michel Foucault that is perhaps less well-known yet more applicable, as least from the practicing novelist's viewpoint.

Barthes begins with a sentence from Balzac's "Sarrasine," in which a narrator comments on the thoughts of a castrato disguised as a woman. Barthes then wonders who is speaking: the hero? The Balzac who is thinking of his own experience with women? The authorial Balzac who is compelled to say something literary? A universal voice? The voice of romantic psychology? "We shall never know," says Barthes, "for the good reason that writing is the destruction of every voice, of every point of origin."

From this promising and pointedly analytical beginning Barthes

descends into an impressionistic dismissiveness, referring to a creature called "the scriptor" who succeeds the author and who has
neither "passions, humors, feelings, impressions" but rather an
"immense dictionary from which he draws a writing that can know
no halt; life never does more than imitate the book, and the book
itself is only a tissue of signs." Or, as Derrida says, *il n'y a pas de hors-
texte*. It would be possible, of course, to think that, if there is indeed
nothing outside the text, then at least writers are free to write the
text themselves. But as Robert Scholes says, an author is not "a
fully unified individuality [*sic*] freely making esthetic choices."

Foucault extends the best of Barthes's argument in an essay entitled "What Is an Author?" (1969). It will not do to "repeat the
empty affirmation that the author has disappeared," says Foucault;
"instead, we must locate the space left empty by the author's disappearance, follow the distribution of gaps and breaches, and watch
for the openings that this disappearance uncovers." After all, "Everyone knows that, in a novel narrated in the first person, neither
the first person pronoun, nor the present indicative refer
exactly either to the writer or to the moment in which he writes,
but rather to an alter ego whose distance from the author varies,
often changing in the course of the work." Coining the phrase
"author-function," Foucault offers a somewhat inelegant yet useful substitute for Barthes's "scriptor": "It would be just as wrong
to equate the author with the real writer as to equate him with
the fictitious speaker; the author-function is carried out and operates in the scission itself, in this division and distance." Somewhere
between author Herman Melville and his narrator Ishmael is the
author-function that wrote *Moby-Dick*, then.

An important corollary to deconstruction's assertion that writing is more intertextual *pastiche* than authorial creation is the belief that all writing, especially realism, is inherently repressive and
supportive of established power. In *Tristes Tropiques* (1955), for
example, Claude Lévi-Strauss argues that "the primary function

of written communication is to facilitate slavery." Louis Althusser identifies "good books," in his essay "Ideology and Ideological State Apparatuses" (1970), as similar in function to the family, the army, and the church, all mechanisms that assist the state in self-replication. The realistic novel is an especially repressive tool, as Catherine Belsay says in *Critical Practice* (1980), because it reproduces reality without questioning it. And in *The Novel and the Police* (1988), D. A. Miller calls Anthony Trollope, usually considered the most genteel of novelists, "terroristic" in his implicit approval of Victorian behavior. Clearly there is a sharp distinction between the attitudes of these critics and those who still find reading a liberating activity.

In recent years, many critics dissatisfied with what they see as the closed and private world of deconstructive readings have taken up the New Historicism, which, in opposition to traditional historiography, tends to look beyond the names of politicians and dates of battles to discover the "true," hidden, and often subversive history that gives shape to literature. A New Historical reading of Henry James's *Portrait of a Lady* (1881), for example, might focus on the ways in which nineteenth-century economic trends shaped the novel. Though the Civil War had settled the question of overt ownership of human beings, the rise of monopoly capitalism made the buying and selling of labor power, of men and women, more prevalent; thinkers as diverse as Henry David Thoreau and Karl Marx argued against the suppression of the individual under industrial capitalism. In his preface to *Portrait*, James allies himself with capitalism by depicting the writer as a businessman trafficking in the products he creates. James is the owner, then, of his characters and speaks in his preface of the joy of "possession." Yet, a New Historical reader might point out, he also negates his self-presentation of the writer as capitalist. James is too much the partisan of Isabel Archer and the enemy of her controlling husband, Gilbert Osmond, to be comfortable with his own image as owner and manipulator of others, and this authorial ambivalence shows in the novel's in-conclusive finish.

Another important twentieth-century school of criticism is reader-response criticism, which focuses on neither the author nor the text but the reader. Reader-response can be so subjective that it is sometimes called the anti-theory of literary theories; for that reason, many critics inclined in this direction prefer what they call reader-reception theory, which goes beyond one person's response to examine how an ideal reader should respond to a given text. For example, in *The Act of Reading* (1976), Wolfgang Iser argues that a novel is "constituted" by a reader who fills in "blanks" left by the novelist; seeking to neither bore nor distress the reader, the novelist leaves gaps for the reader to account for, thus ensuring the reader's full and pleasurable participation.

The erasure of the author, one of deconstruction's central tenets, has been received with varying degrees of cordiality in the United States. Paul de Man's *Blindness and Insight* (1971) supports the idea that fiction is total artifice, cut off from any moral or even represen-tational value. But de Man was a Belgian émigré, one who turned out to have an unsavory past with Nazi connections, as David Leh-man points out in *Sign of the Times: Deconstruction and the Fall of Paul de Man* (1991). A Yale colleague of de Man and a critic with ties to deconstruction—yet one too various in his interpre-tive approaches to be comfortable in any single niche—is Harold Bloom, whose influential *Anxiety of Influence* (1973) argues that each writer is a Freudian misreader of his literary ancestors, mak-ing new books from his misunderstandings of previous ones.

Predictably, many American feminist critics, "queer theory" spe-cialists, African American critics, and others concerned with gen-der, sexual orientation, race, and ethnicity are resistant to the idea that there is no such thing as a self. Kate Millet's *Sexual Politics* (1970) is a visceral response to the sexism of male novelists such as Henry Miller and Norman Mailer, a line of argument furthered by Sandra Gilbert and Susan Gubar in *The Madwoman in the Attic* (1979), whose dominant image is of woman marginalized, as Mrs. Rochester is by her controlling husband in Charlotte Brontë's *Jane Eyre* (1847). In France, Julia Kristeva and Hélène Cixous have built on Lacan's reading of Freud to develop a feminist criticism that promotes the linking of female sexuality with creative openness.

Of course, just as "masculinist" readings have generated feminist ones, so, too, has an anti-feminist approach evolved, most notably in the writings of Camille Paglia, whose scholarly *Sexual Personae: Art and Decadence from Nefertiti to Emily Dickinson* (1990) is now probably less well-known than the popularly oriented *Vamps and Tramps: New Essays* (1994). A diehard Madonna fan, Paglia presents herself as a pro-pornography lesbian who nonetheless recommends Jane Austen novels over the current crop of what she describes as "crappy lesbian movies." Prominent African American critics include Darwin T. Turner, Houston A. Baker, the Toni Morrison known best for her novels but also the author of *Playing in the Dark: Whiteness and the Literary Imagination* (1992), and Henry Louis Gates Jr., author of the groundbreaking *Signifying Monkey: A Theory of Afro-American Literary Criticism* (1988) and the critic largely responsible for re-popularizing Zora Neale Hurston's *Their Eyes Were Watching God* (1937). There is even a return, if not to the hidebound conservatism of the New Humanists, at least to a concern with values in books like novelist John Gardner's *On Moral Fiction* (1978).

Thus criticism is too diverse in the last years of the twentieth century to be restricted only to "theory," with its narrow French poststructuralist implications, even though manuscripts are turned down by university presses every day and job candidates rejected for being insufficiently "theoretical." An air of religious fundamentalism characterizes the hardcore cadre described by moderates as "theory heads," an all-or-nothing group who have little patience with those who want to take from theory what they find useful and retain a healthy skepticism toward the rest.

For better or worse, history may favor the moderate critics in a world where education is universal, information cheap, and consumers prone to eclecticism. Barriers are dissolving everywhere in a world where a man of, say, Swedish American descent and his Japanese-Hispanic lover can order a "Hawai'ian" pizza with pineapple and ham and spend the evening watching satellite TV, surfing from eco-tourism documentaries to country-music videos in which black-hatted guitar twangers stroll Caribbean beaches, arm in arm with bikini-clad starlets. Predictably, criticism is becoming eclectic and highly personal as well. Indeed, there is a so-called *moi* criticism, which includes works like Frank Lentricchia's *The Edge of Night* (1994) and Eve Kosofsky Sedgwick's *Tendencies* (1994). These critics combine literary criticism with the self-advertisement condemned (even if often practiced) by old-school deconstructionists. These two authors, like others of this only somewhat facetiously titled school, are serious and self-indulgent at the same time. Mainly, though, they dramatize the vital role of the living, breathing reader in any literary transaction, a role too often overlooked in the proliferation of arcane systems.

What Is a Critic?

The sign outside the lecture hall read "The Language of Criticism and the Sciences of Man." It was 1966, and, like my fellow Johns Hopkins graduate students, I was out of it. (Later I would hear one of them cry, "Would somebody please tell me what structuralism is so I'll know if I'm a structuralist or not?") But I was drawn to the symposium by several considerations: the desire to better myself professionally, a provincial youth's interest in anything billed as "international," and, not least, the hope that my professors would see me there.

The talk I had decided to attend was to be given by the Marxist Lucien Goldmann, about whom I knew nothing. But I liked his name; it sounded like the name of a James Bond villain. A few days before I had read an article on innocence and experience in the works of my favorite novelist, Henry James, by a scholar named Lotus Snow, whose name sounded like that of a Bond heroine. If I went to hear Lucien Goldmann, perhaps Lotus Snow would be there as well. Maybe Lucien would introduce me to Lotus. Better yet, maybe Lucien would try to practice his Marxist wiles on Lotus (the Cold War was on, remember), and I would save her. "Oh, David," she would sigh. . . .

A revolution was going on, and I was dreaming of Lotus Snow. The Johns Hopkins symposium was the historical event that, in the course of a few days, changed permanently the reading, teaching, and writing of literature in this country. In that instance, the

Hopkins campus became the Plymouth Rock for that amalgam of Saussurean strategies most economically called "theory," and most of the founding fathers were there: Goldmann (of whose talk I remember nothing), Roland Barthes, Jacques Lacan, Tzvetan Todorov.

And towering above them all, or so it seems in retrospect, was Jacques Derrida, the high priest of deconstruction, who gave a talk entitled "Structure, Sign, and Play in the Discourse of the Human Sciences." It was here that many American academics learned for the first time that a literary text was no longer simply a well-made novel or poem or play but an impersonal skein of arbitrary linguistic codes. That meant a new way of reading: if the text has no author-imposed structure, even though it claims to—or especially because it claims to—then the critic's task is a pitiless subversion of that false claim.

At the time, the indeterminacy of texts was big news to virtually everyone, including me. I had just arrived in Baltimore a few months before from Baton Rouge; at Louisiana State University, where I had taken my undergraduate degree, the spirit of the New Criticism was still strong. Cleanth Brooks and Robert Penn Warren had long since departed for Yale, but the idea of a poem as an autonomous formal construct with a single derivable meaning hadn't really changed.

I wasn't intransigent about the theorists' insistence on the indeterminacy of meaning; indeed, already I had abandoned much of my homegrown New Criticism for headier continental approaches. My most dazzling Hopkins professor was J. Hillis Miller, then a respected phenomenologist rapidly becoming celebrity deconstructionist. After I left Miller's lectures in Gilman Hall, I had to walk through a little patch of woods to get to my room in Wolman Hall, and in good weather I used to sit on a fallen tree there and reread my notes, happy that minds like Miller's existed and confident that I could have one just as classy if I only applied myself.

There was a bar on Greenmount Street that served twenty-cent highballs on Wednesday nights; penny-wise grad students would moisten their clay there, shoulder to shoulder with the more routine customers. Once I explained to a morose regular that life *was* worth living, that even though his wife had left him and his kids had turned out to be disappointments and he'd just been laid off from his job at the McCormick spice factory, none of that mattered because the human mind was so, uh, mental.

2. LUNCH AT WILL'S GRILL

As you walk into the lavish Carolyn Blount Theatre in Montgomery, home of the Alabama Shakespeare Festival, you notice a life-size statue of the playwright looking prosperous yet humble, as befits one so venerated. You pick up your ticket, which you reserved earlier by calling 277-BARD. Since you have a few minutes and feel a mite peckish, you have a sandwich at the snack bar, which is called Will's Grill. As you lunch at Will's Grill, you contemplate joining Will's Guild, the two hundred–plus volunteer group that provides much of the support for the ASF. In doing so, you are joined by countless others—not just in Montgomery, but in cities like Cedar City, Utah, and Lakewood, Ohio, for there are more than thirty year-round theater companies for whom Shakespeare is the core repertory.

While Shakespeare is either dead or semi-dead in the seminar room, then, depending on whether you are a Barthesian (and believe that the author is totally extinct) or a Foucauldian (and think novelists, playwrights, and poets are just sort of staggering through their careers like Frankenstein's monster), he is growing healthier every day in towns like Montgomery, Cedar City, and Lakewood. And rightly so, says the would-be Shakespeare just down the hall in the writing workshop. In the *Introductory Lectures on Psycho-Analysis,* Freud says the artist wants "honor, power, riches, fame,

and the love of women"; change that last noun to "men" or simply "others," and most artists would agree. Writers especially are
prone to ascribe to themselves motives that are both lofty and ambitious; Marjorie Perloff quotes Philip Levine as saying that "a true
writer . . . wants the power to say what's in his [*sic*] mind or heart
and say it so it will last forever" (*AWP Newsletter*, December 1987).

But then Perloff lashes Levine with that special kind of fury that
the initiated reserve for the naive. Doesn't Levine know that "any
contemporary theorist, whether Derridean or Lacanian or of the
Frankfurt School or French feminist, would say, 'what's in his mind
or heart' is not *his* to begin with; it has been planted there by the
language he/she uses, the dominant ideology of the culture, the
moment in history in which he/she writes"? Overlooking Philip
Levine's implacable opposition to "the dominant ideology of the
culture" in virtually everything he has written, Perloff also chas-
tises him for his chutzpah in hoping that his utterances will last
forever.

Yet do not Derrida and the others crave honor, immortality, and
so on? Perloff attributes the rise of theory to "the post-War ethos"
that "undermined the religious and ethical pieties that had made
the New Criticism possible." In doing so, she wraps herself in the
flag: the vanquished New Critics were pious hypocrites, whereas
the victorious theory people are fearless truth-seekers.

Something curious is going on here: even though Perloff lashes
poet Levine with undue severity, for some reason she identifies,
not poets as a group, but the New Critics and their cold-warrior
sycophants as the real enemy. This theory-versus–New Criticism
formula is accepted unquestioningly these days; for example, Malcolm Bradbury confirms it in the newspaper of record when he says
that "in the '60s and '70s, deconstruction filled—perhaps better,
emptied—the gap left in the American humanities by the demise
of the Old New Criticism" (*New York Times Book Review*, February
24, 1991). Today this scenario is universally accepted: that a cadre of

lean, mean theorists hit the silk over campus one sunny afternoon, landed, folded their chutes, beat down the doors with their rifle butts, and routed the New Critical troops, who were too fusty to know what hit them.

But official history, like any other text, can be read several ways. Take Perloff's particular account. Perloff mentions theory's supposed enemy, the New Critics, only briefly and impersonally; curiously, she then singles out, not a New Critic, but a poet for her most caustic attack. Now one of the tenets of deconstruction is that the position the writer is trying to repress will recur as a hidden motif in her writing. To Perloff, then, the natural enemy of the theorist is not the New Critic but the poet. And in vintage Freudian fashion, the theorist and the poet are enemies not because they are different but because they are identical.

The history of this idea—that theorists and artists are indistinguishable—is a formidable one. Centuries ago, Montaigne described philosophy as sophisticated poetry, and from Montaigne's position it is but a short step to that of Paul de Man, the foremost deconstructor in the United States until his posthumous disgrace, who wrote (in *Blindness and Insight*) that "the relationship between author and critic does not designate a difference in the type of activity involved." Similar statements by contemporary observers confirm Montaigne's bold dictum and de Man's diffident reformulation: theory is itself "a serious contemporary aesthetics" (Bradbury, *TLS*, January 17, 1992), and "deconstructionist writing . . . constitutes a body of literature" (Nathaniel Laor, *Yale French Studies*, November 1990). And if theoretical texts read the way poems and stories do, then it follows that an author is an author, even if there is no such thing: in his biography of Michel Foucault, Didier Eribon quotes the brilliant, volatile author of *Histoire de la folie* as saying, "To speak of madness one must have the talent of a poet," to which the historian of science Georges Canguilhem replies, "But you, sir, have it."

Today resourceful professors make connections between theoretical texts and creative works: Paul Berman equates the new strategies with "*Finnegans Wake* or canvases by Mark Rothko" (*Tikkun*, January–February 1992), and even Perloff has students read Derrida's *Glas* alongside John Ashbery's "Litany" and John Cage's *Roaratorio*. Such statements suggest a cooperation between theory and writing or at least nothing more sinister than a healthy competition, which is how it should be: theory needs writing to practice on, writing needs theory to call it to account. Forget the New Criticism; the only love-hate relationship worth talking about is the one between theory and writing.

The truth is that the New Criticism was murdered, not by a SWAT team of Paris theoreticians, but by sheer demographics. The Cold War collapsed, and the baby boomers, emboldened by new music, new drugs, new sexual practices, and, most important of all, new disdain for their elders, found better things to do than reread the same old dusty masterpieces. Up sprang new disciplines: creative writing, women's studies, minority studies. And of these three, creative writing grew the most rapidly. Enrollments boomed in writing workshops—why read someone else's poems when you could write your own? And instead of writing critical papers to read to an unappreciative audience at the Modern Language Association meeting, literature professors began writing novels and traveling around the country to give readings at a thousand dollars a pop. By doing so, the new professor/writers were using their new celebrity simultaneously to occupy the center of the English department—who, after all, was more noticeable than they?—and to rise above it, since they were so often absent.

Thus the professor/writers jetted in and out, got their pictures in the paper, and were as much admired afar as they were detested at home. The way was clear for the savvy professor/critic, then: emulate the example of the abhorrent and adored professor/writer. The New Critical model—or, more precisely, the model of the New Critic—was of no strategic value to the professor/critic who, like the professor/writer, wanted simultaneously to take over and transcend the English department. The New Critics wanted to disappear into the study of literature; their model of an English department was a factory in which dozens of patient workers, guided by training and common sense, dismantled texts and put them back together again. And if the workers required supervisors, these tended to be fastidious, retiring types like John Crowe Ransom and Cleanth Brooks. Stars were needed, and so stars appeared in the east: as creative writing—not theory—plowed under the New Criticism in the late sixties, the European mages arrived in the unlikely city of Baltimore in the nick of time. On that day the critic died, and the theorist was born. In the lobby, the writer was waiting, dagger concealed in a bouquet.

Today, almost anything that can be said about writing can be said about theory as well. Both are anti-hierarchical. Both deny the validity of a monopoly viewpoint. Both concede an inherent subjectivity in everything. Both are playful—the colorless sobriety of the New Critics has been replaced by the antics of theorists as devoted as any poet to epigrams, puns, put-ons, jokes, and neologisms.

With all this in common, naturally the two disciplines share one more attribute: each hates the other. The theorist's contempt for the writer is readily apparent in essays like "The Death of the Author" and statements like Jonathan Culler's triumphant proclamation (in *Framing the Sign*) that "the history of literature now becomes part of the history of criticism." And the feeling is mutual—since most creative writers devote themselves to poems and stories instead of essays, the stunning anti-intellectualism of many creative writers is less a matter of record, yet widely published authors of my acquaintance have rebuffed attempts to discuss theoretical issues with statements like "I don't believe in any of that" and "I'm surprised you feel obliged to read that stuff." Barthes and Culler may set writers' teeth on edge, but their arrogance is matched by that of poets and novelists who greet theorists' best efforts with dismissive sarcasm.

Roland Barthes notwithstanding, one more attribute theorists share with writers is the belief that—at least in their own cases—the author is not only very much alive but also deserving of the kind of veneration once reserved for the sages they themselves have deposed. I saw Michel Foucault outside a Paris movie theater in 1978; with his shaved head and signature white turtleneck, he was as different in appearance from his followers as those Martian scientists who come to earth in science fiction to lord it over the rest of us. In the crush that surrounded him, his admirers clawed him like tigers.

3. TURF NAZIS MUST DIE

Paul de Man's memorial service in the Yale Art Gallery in January 1984 is another example of over-the-top lionizing of a theorist, especially in light of de Man's futile efforts to divert attention from himself and his shameful past. Walter Kendrick quotes rhapsodic eulogies by J. Hillis Miller, Peter Brooks, Geoffrey Hartman, and other celebrity theorists, the most egregious of whom is the Shoshana Felman who says, "I felt that through him, through his works and through his person, something extraordinary spoke. . . . Such was the power of his extraordinary mind. Such was the power of his extraordinary heart" (*Voice Literary Supplement*, April 1988). Three years later, it was revealed that this extraordinary mind and heart had written some 170 articles for collaborationist newspapers in wartime Belgium. In David Lehman's book *Signs of the Times: Deconstruction and the Fall of Paul de Man* and in shorter pieces by Kendrick and Jon Wiener (*Nation*, January 9, 1988), de Man is seen as doing little more than celebrating the cultural appropriateness of Nazism, although in one article he actually advocates the shipping of Europe's Jews to an island.

Of course, these revelations don't really discredit deconstruction or any other theory. If it works, it works, no matter who thought it up. These sensational exposés are meaningless—unless, of course, other theorists turn out to be Nazis, too. . . .

Well, there *is* Martin Heidegger, Derrida's major influence and an academic whose career advanced as a direct result of his collaboration with the Nazi authorities. And Hans Robert Jauss, a specialist in the aesthetics of reception now known to have served in the S.S. And Julia Kristeva, whose *Powers of Horror* is described by Juliet MacCannell as "a theoretical *justification* for the holocaust" (*Semiotica*, 1986). And Jacques Lacan, in whom Jeffrey Mehlman (*SubStance*, 1982) sees the potential for anti-Semitism when Lacan, in *Four Fundamental Concepts of Psycho-Analysis*, makes ambiguous use of Léon Bloy's comparison of Freud to some repulsive old Jewish merchants. Still other observers take theorists to task for failing to live up to the progressive social program that their canon-breaking implies: Elizabeth Wilson accuses Kristeva of elitism (*New Statesman and Society*, June 14, 1991), and James Snead takes on just about everybody in an article called "Racist Traces in Postmodernist Theory and Literature" (*Critical Quarterly*, spring 1991).

The de Man revelations had the anti-theorists rubbing their hands with glee, writing I-told-you-so letters to the *New York Review of Books* and warning their graduate students about fascist colleagues. Wait a minute, though. Unfortunately, bias is an equal-opportunity vice, and no writer has any business saying that Nazism is endemic to theory. After all, the portrayal of Jews in Western literature is hardly something for writers to be proud of. Anti-Semitism in Chaucer's "Prioress's Tale," Shakespeare's *The Merchant of Venice*, Marlowe's *The Jew of Malta*, Dickens's *Oliver Twist*, and works by such modernists as Pound, Eliot, Fitzgerald, and Hemingway amount to a genuine roll call of shame. And these are instances of only one form of bias; literary works disfigured by misogyny and racism are far greater in number than anything the theorists have produced.

Theory does not make bigots of people, then, and neither does poetry. Yet why do theorists and writers alike often seem peremptory, arrogant, and authoritarian? The enemy is not Nazism but romanticism, of which Nazism is simply one particularly visible and repellent type. When Hitler spoke of killing reason, when he boasted of marching to his goal like a somnambulist and intoxicated himself and his audiences with megalomaniacal dreams, he wore the Nazi uniform but he spoke a far older and more universal language. In its positive form, romanticism can be liberating, transcendent, compassionate, generous. But I speak here of romanticism's dark side, its capacity for a self-worshipping ruthlessness. As Bertrand Russell writes in his introduction to *A History of Western Philosophy*, "Tigers are more beautiful than sheep, but we prefer them behind bars. The typical romantic removes the bars and enjoys the magnificent leaps with which the tiger annihilates the sheep. He exhorts men to imagine themselves tigers, and when he succeeds the results are not wholly pleasant." Academic tigers may not be as bloodthirsty as the ones Russell describes. But the terms are useful: if you think of yourself as a tiger, sooner or later your colleagues are going to start to look like sheep. The next thing you know, you're posting "Tigers Only" signs in the halls.

Turf wars are natural when one group begins to imagine itself superior to another, especially if the other group feels the same way. But turf wars are not inevitable. The alternative to a bloody-minded romanticism is what Michel Foucault might describe as a dialectical power, a compromise so subtle, as I argue in the following essay, that it must be constantly reexamined by all parties. True, this dialectical power is not as dizzying as a collective Hitlerian brain spasm. But it is indispensable to the health of an intellectual community.

In the meantime, faculty who care about these things must remember that it is our students who count, not how much turf we control. One hears of entire faculties being paralyzed by theory wars. What do these people think they were hired to do? Students want to be taught, not watch writers and theorists slug it out like blindfolded prizefighters on roller skates. If we are going to be ruthless, let us be ruthless in our intolerance of intolerance. And just as important, let us make sure we do not locate intolerance where it does not exist.

And surely an English professor needn't be either a "theorist" or a "fool," to use the terms of John L'Heureux's academic satire *The Handmaid of Desire*. Indeed, that book examines the life of a fictional Mistah Kurtz, who is a fearful, embattled theorist on the one hand, a closet reader of novels on the other, and, because of this insupportable conflict, a candidate for early stroke. The real Mistah Kurtzes of the world would have healthier lives if they did what physicists do: perform research at the highest level and teach their grad students and physics majors to do the same but also offer Physics for Nonmajors classes and host Physics Day for the community on Saturday mornings. Similarly, classical music operates on two levels these days; there will always be the performer who simply plays and then backs offstage bowing, but now there are musicians who stop to make comments between selections, ask children to come up and sit around the piano during the encore, and so on. If English professors choose to stay proudly arcane and to remain aloof from the Great Conversation, it seems to me that they do so at their own peril.

Mr. Post-Everything

THE LIFE AND TIMES OF
LEOPOLD VON SACHER-MASOCH

To read any of Leopold Ritter von Sacher-Masoch's novels is to recall the question that the cheerful student is said to have asked Robert Frost after a poetry reading: "Mr. Frost, is that a real poem, or did you just make it up?" Overlooking for a moment the fine distinctions that question fails to assume, let us say simply, no, Masoch didn't "make up" his wild tales of men who dressed up like bears and bandits and the women who pursued them, bound them, and whipped them unconscious. His heroes did—or had done to them—the things Masoch knew and loved best. And yet he was so much more than they were. As an author, Masoch is known almost entirely for *Venus in Furs*, though in fact he was the author of many works on a variety of subjects. To discern what Masoch offers today's reader, it is necessary to understand not only the precise nature of his masochistic schemes but also their connection to the larger world of culture and politics.

Masoch was born in 1835 in Lemberg, the capital of Galicia, in the northeast corner of the Austro-Hungarian Empire, near the Polish and Russian borders. Then as now, the population of Galicia was one of the most mixed in Europe. It consisted of a peasant stock, variously known as Ukrainians, Little Russians, or Ruthenians, who had endured centuries of serfdom; the mainly Polish landowners; predominately urban Jews; an official Austrian aristocracy; and the Germans, Hungarians, Bohemians, Rumanians, and Armenians who made up the rest of the populace, each group with its own agendas and resentments.

An incident described in James Cleugh's admittedly overdramatized biography (yet the only widely available one) is illustrative. In 1846 the Galician Poles decided to revolt against their Austrian masters, and one of the more fantastic plots was for Galician women to entice their Austrian dancing partners to a military ball in Lemberg and slip their heads into wire nooses as part of some allegorical charade, whereupon a signal was to be given and the oppressors strangled en masse. A death in the Hapsburg family resulted in the cancellation of a temporary ban on social functions for army officers, but the rest of the revolt began as planned, even though the peasants, more interested in revenge than in political autonomy, began to settle old scores with the landowners, who were, to quote Cleugh, "beaten to death with flails, beheaded with scythes, nailed like foxes or owls to the doors of barns or flung into anthills with legs and arms broken and heads smeared with honey." During this period, Masoch's father was the chief of police in Lemberg, which put Masoch at the center of some heady action during his most impressionable years. During the revolutionary year of 1848, the father was transferred to Prague, and Masoch recalled being on the police barricades with an older girl cousin named Miroslava who wore a fur jacket and carried pistols in her belt. She shouted commands and ordered Leopold about; Cleugh notes that "amid these episodes of death and destruction he conceived a passionate adoration of her."

Masoch's influences weren't entirely historical, however. Some of his most formative experiences involved his paternal aunt, the Countess Zenobia. One day, during a game of hide and seek, Masoch concealed himself from the other children in Zenobia's wardrobe. Then the door of her bedroom opened, and, as Masoch watched through the keyhole, Zenobia entered along with a handsome stranger. The two lay down on a divan and began to exchange caresses. At the height of this reckless behavior, the Count himself appeared. Instead of fleeing shamefacedly, however, Zenobia drew herself up and struck her husband in the mouth, drawing blood. The Count fled through one door, the cowardly lover through another. An overexcited Masoch caused the wardrobe to creak in his excitement, and his aunt dragged him forth to rain blows on his anguished posterior. Nearly forty years later, Masoch recalled in an essay: "I must admit that while I writhed under my aunt's cruel blows, I experienced acute pleasure."

From the actions of the bloodthirsty belles of Lemberg to those of the redoubtable Zenobia, one conclusion was inevitable for the young Masoch. Cleugh quotes "an anonymous student of Galicia" who wrote in 1848 ("the year of so many revolutions") that "the women in this land have only one choice. Either they fully dominate the husband and make him their slave, which is their most usual behavior, or else they themselves sink to the most pitiable level of abject existence." Or, as the narrator of *Venus in Furs* says, "One person must be the hammer, the other, the anvil."

But then the narrator adds, "I choose to be the anvil." The road to an understanding of any sexual pathology never runs smooth, and theories of the etiology of masochism abound, often contradicting one another. One classic explanation is that the masochist is actually struggling to minimize his suffering; the boy who hoists his rump in the air knows that his mother will greet the rude gesture with a slap, but isn't a slap preferable to castration? Gilles Deleuze's contribution involves a definition by opposition in which masochism is shown to have absolutely nothing to do with the sadism with which it is often and spuriously linked.

To Deleuze, the worlds of sadism and masochism simply do not communicate. A sadist would never beat a masochist; if your intention is to inflict pain, why whip someone who enjoys it? But because masochism has been studied less than sadism—or Masoch less than

Sade, who is one of the darlings of poststructuralists—what is less known but equally true is that the masochist doesn't want to be punished by a sadist. There is no fun in being thrashed by some-one who enjoys it. The masochist's control consists in the enlisting of an *unwilling* party to do the rough stuff. You can't corrupt the corrupted; you can't "educate" someone already well-schooled in the science of pain.

Politically, the differences between sadism and masochism are just as stark. The sadist seizes and possesses his victims; the maso-chist creates alliances with them. The sadist wants quantity, repe-tition, the piling of victim upon victim; the masochist seeks qual-ity and therefore searches painstakingly for a single person whom he can educate and persuade. This difference can be seen in the attitudes the two types take toward the written word. The sadist despises contracts—despots don't need them. Yet the masochist loves contracts, since they guarantee a long-lived and equable re-lationship (in his life as in his fiction, Masoch placed newspaper advertisements spelling out his requirements and also signed de-tailed contracts with his abusive paramours). Deleuze makes a use-ful distinction between pornography, which is descriptive (literally "graphic"), and pornology, or discourse that is logocentric rather than pictorial.

After all, in the world of the masochist what one does mainly is wait. The first time I read *Venus in Furs* I was in my teens, and I remember wondering, "Where's the good stuff?" *Venus* is pretty decent—pretty boring, actually. There is little for the cen-sor to strike, unless, as Deleuze says, "he were to question a cer-tain atmosphere of suffocation and suspense which is a feature of all of Masoch's novels." Whereas the sadist invades, overpow-ers, and seeks to prolong his domination for as long as possible, for the masochist the relationship is tenuous at every moment. The masochist must make his tormentor love her work but not too much. (Masoch's "victims" are male, their tormentors female;

ordinarily one avoids the masculine pronoun, but if ever it were justified, here is the occasion.) Otherwise, his beloved would become
a sadist and alter the terms of the relationship. In *Venus in Furs,*
Wanda, the Venus-figure, warns the narrator about this possibility
by means of an instructive fable:

> "Do you know the story of the ox of Dionysius?" she asked.
>
> "I remember it vaguely. Why?"
>
> "A courtier invented a new instrument of torture for the tyrant
> of Syracuse. The victim was to be put inside a hollow bronze ox
> under which a fire was to be lit. It was intended that as the metal
> grew hot the prisoner would howl with pain and thus imitate the
> bellowing of an ox. Dionysius expressed interest in the invention
> and decided to try it out on the spot; so he had the inventor himself
> placed inside the ox. A very instructive story. It is you who have
> taught me selfishness, pride and cruelty, and you shall be my first
> victim."

The sadist's art consists in thinking up new and more exquisite
sufferings for the victim who is already under his control. But the
masochist's art is more subtle, since it consists of controlling someone who must have the illusion of her own freedom. One reason
why Sade may be of more interest to scholars than Masoch is that
the sadist, however contemptible, at least represents the active
principle, whereas the masochist is merely passive. But the masochist's activity is concealed, his empowering of his partner decep-
tive. The twin dangers of masochism are that the masochist might
fail by affronting his would-be accomplice and driving her away or
succeed too well by bringing out the Dionysius in her.

Another distinction Deleuze makes is between the irony of Sade
and the humor of Masoch. Sade pays the state the ultimate compli-
ment by aping its power and its apathy toward its victims. Masoch,
on the other hand, wants to deny the power of others and then dis-
solves in laughter when he realizes his helplessness; throughout his

writing, he has his narrators say, whenever they get into a particular pickle, something along the lines of, "I would have laughed if I hadn't felt so humiliated." Actually, a political censor would find more to delete in Masoch than a sexual censor—kings don't like to be laughed at. Whereas the sadist is all superego and can only find an ego externally, the terms are reversed for the masochist; in masochism the ego is laughing at the external superego it has created and thus has power over, regardless of how it looks to anyone else.

Noting that the two men wrote in the contexts of the revolutions of 1789 and 1848, Deleuze points out that "fundamental problems of rights begin to emerge in their true light even as they become perverted in the work of Sade and Masoch and turned into literary elements in a parody of the philosophy of history." And that may be the ultimate value of these two authors—that separately they teach us about specific clinical conditions, yes, but together they speak eloquently about the workings of power, be it in the statehouse or on the page.

In all but the clinical sense, the act of reading is masochistic; the writer seeks the attention of the otherwise indifferent reader, seeks to control and manipulate while allowing the reader a false sense of autonomy. That is why the first few pages of the novel are crucial; here is where the terms of the contract are presented, this is where the reader either signs and thereby agrees to an alliance of a certain duration or goes away affronted.

Venus in Furs begins with a shocking scene of dominance: a voluptuary is about to be trampled underfoot by a fur-wrapped "goddess of Love." Immediately, though, the reader is distanced from any unsavory connotations, for the scene turns out to be nothing more than "a very curious dream." Further, the dream turns out to have a high-art basis; as the narrator recounts the story to his friend Severin, his attention is drawn to a copy of Titian's *Venus with the Mirror* that has clearly prompted his fantasy. Besides, the story of *Venus in Furs* is really Severin's story—as the two friends explore their mutual feelings toward masochistic pleasures, Severin produces a diary.

Through a series of complicated enticements and reversals, Masoch manipulates the reader so that he is utterly under the author's control yet utterly convinced of his freedom. (Again, because *Venus in Furs* is a kind of handbook for men who want to deceive women into mistreating them, we must assume that Masoch is writing for a masculine reader. Oh, but clever author! Wily Masoch also feminizes his masculine reader in order to get "her" to do his will.) First comes the naughty story; then the revelation that "it is only a dream," which allows the reader to enjoy and disavow the fantasy simultaneously; then the high-art connection that suggests the dreamer is in exalted company and therefore needn't disavow the dream; and then the found-manuscript ploy, which encourages the reader/dreamer to displace any lingering guilt onto Severin, for it is he, as it turns out, who is the naughty fellow, not the original narrator and certainly not the reader.

At this point, that reader has either abandoned the book or not; if not, then simultaneously he is and isn't a masochist. This deliberate confusion is compounded by the fact that the narrator invites identification by speaking in the first person, and even though he relinquishes the narration to Severin, Severin too speaks in his own voice, so that the identification is not only doubled but deepened—we are encouraged to identify first with the mere fantasist and then with the character who has made the fantasy real. And then Titian is brought in to legitimize the reader's masochistic tendencies, so that by the time the diary gets under way, the reader cannot be blamed for feelings of repulsion ("I really don't want a muscular woman to beat me") and acceptance ("maybe these feelings are more universal than I thought").

Furthermore, Severin is not interested in merely being used and discarded (the reader will see here how easy it is to be convinced of the masochist's submissiveness—I should have written "Severin is

not interested in merely using and discarding someone"). As much
as any conventional hero, he is looking for love; when he meets
Wanda, they agree that if, over the course of a year, they find they
are suited to each other, then they will marry; in the meantime,
they will live together as husband and wife. Well, not really—
this is Masoch, after all, so living together means that when they
travel, she rides in the first-class carriage while he rides in third-
class with the riffraff. And when she finally gets around to flailing
him (remember that since the masochist wants to be beaten, it is
the withholding that is painful to him), she sends him to work in
the garden for a month like a servant. Again the deliberate confusion of the reader—Severin is "sick," yet he wants love the way
"normal" people do.

Should the reader tire of Masoch's manipulations, he can simply
put the book down, but by this point, that seems unlikely. As Severin thinks to himself, "The comic side of my situation is that I can
escape but do not want to; I am ready to endure anything as soon
as she threatens to set me free." Again, to return to my teenage
reading of *Venus in Furs*, I remember being uneasy then because
I wondered if this was what sexual relations between adults were
like; this time I felt uneasy because I realized that Masoch was describing what relations between writer and reader were like and
how much I, as reader, surrendered every time I opened a book—
any book.

In his nonliterary life, Masoch seems to have been a more or
less exemplary citizen. He was reserved, even shy, even though
he had a reputation for kindness toward children, animals, and
the less fortunate. Perhaps most remarkable of all, he was a philo-
Semite; coming from a region where any disruption of the social
order served as an excuse for a bloody pogrom, Masoch not only
championed Jewish rights but also made the underdog status of
the Galician Jews the starting point for his utopian schemes.

For Masoch was a reformer as much as he was, to use his own
term, a "supersensualist." He never tired of being whipped—often

"on doctor's orders," as he said, the way someone else might take a daily dose of medicine—yet his carnal desires were but a small part of a grand design, the end of which was an ideal world imbued with altruism and Christian principles. His unfinished magnum opus was a vast work called *The Legacy of Cain*. It had six parts entitled *Love, Property, The State, War, Work,* and *Death; Venus in Furs* was one of the six titles included in the *Love* section. Only *Love* and *Property* were finished, but the fragments of *The State* give an idea of Masoch's larger design. There he calls for a United States of Europe, with a fair and uniform legal code replacing the corrupt statutes found even in constitutional governments. And he decries militarism from every standpoint, including the patriotic.

In "The Subject and Power," one of his last essays, Michel Foucault says, "What we need is a new economy of power relations." The essay is included as an afterword in *Michel Foucault: Beyond Structuralism and Hermeneutics,* by Hubert L. Dreyfus and Paul Rabinow, in which the authors suggest that the seminal French thinker's final philosophical position (never articulated) would have looked beyond and perhaps reconciled the opposed claims of structuralism, with its aloof distance, and hermeneutics, with its sense of engagement. This "new economy of power relations" was apparently what Foucault was getting at in the last months of his life. He takes as his text a short article that Kant wrote for the *Berliner Monatschrift* called "Was ist Aufklärung?" or "What does 'Enlightenment' Mean?" Usually considered "a work of relatively small importance," the essay is actually quite significant; whereas Descartes was asking "Who am I?", Kant, in "Was ist Aufklärung?" is asking "What are we?"

The difference between Descartes's position and Kant's is explained by the rise of the state from the sixteenth century forward and the development of a new political structure that simultaneously encourages individuality and totality. And that is what Foucault would have studied had he lived, this "tricky combination in [*sic*] the same political structures of individualization techniques, and of totalization procedures." Foucault knew, like Masoch, that power was dialectical, that it existed not as a static entity or even as "simply a relationship between partners" but as "a way in which certain actions modify others." The imposition of power from above is the sadist's stance, one might argue. The masochist seeks a compromise so subtle that it must be constantly reexamined by both parties; the resulting intimacy all but guarantees a dialectic harmony, at least, if not consensus.

If ever there was a time for dialectic, it is now. In literature, the canon is crumbling; all bets are off. Social scientists are writing essays with titles like "The End of History." Then there are the recent changes in the Soviet bloc. The Moscow McDonald's is now open for business—can Burger King be far behind? (Little Albania alone continues to resist our fast food and all that that entails.) Every day, the world looks more and more like a museum that has just been bombed. Everything that was there before is still there, but it's in pieces now, and the exhibits are jumbled.

When Deleuze observes that in Masoch "history, politics, mysticism, eroticism, nationalism and perversion are closely intermingled," it is hard not to think of that intermingling of literature, politics, sex, linguistics, philosophy, psychology, and just about every other discipline that is variously called poststructural, postmodern—post-everything, as it were. Regardless of one's terminology, the point is that to be fully alive today entails constant motion across new and familiar borders, constant connection-making.

Complex times call for complex people. With his myriad quirks and virtues, Masoch appears to be a person of our era as much as his own, although we won't know until someone writes a critical biography on the scale of Peter Gay's *Freud: A Life for Our Time*. It could be, though, that the thinker who will lead us into the post-everything era was a shy philo-Semite who loved to dress up as a bear.

"The Thing You Can't Explain"

THEORY AND THE UNCONSCIOUS

In 1932, Q. D. Leavis argued in *Fiction and the Reading Public* that an essentially unified readership in the mid–nineteenth century had split into two reading publics by the century's close, an elite that read Henry James and a philistine audience that could aspire no higher than Marie Corelli. Leavis argues for high literature, as she sees it, and against all that is its foe: best-sellers, of course, but also movies, advertising, and that serpent in culture's bosom, radio.

Fiction and the Reading Public thus has all the virtues and vices of any jeremiad. The virtues cluster around Leavis's highly colored and opinionated pronouncements. After all, what good teaching is not pointed, arbitrary, even prejudiced? The vices are found partly in the attitudes that underlie the pronouncements, all of which are hopelessly outdated. What parent would not be overjoyed to see his or her headphone-sprouting teenager hunkered down with *The Sorrows of Satan* or *The Mighty Atom* or any other book by Corelli—any book by anyone, for that matter—rather than sitting glassy eyed before one more death-metal video?

Yet Leavis's biggest mistake is that she sees as permanent a cultural playing field that was paved over long ago, a greensward occupied at various times of the day (but never the same time) by either reedy, insectile Jacobites or else the unbuttoned devotees of Corelli's melodramas. But education is universal now, information cheap, and concrete everywhere. Culture is played out in shopping malls, where bank presidents and belly dancers lick frozen yogurt as they stroll from book shop to record store, pursued by mimes.

Like culture, theory too tends to be a little hyper these days. To take a not-so-extreme example, Susan McClary, in her foreword to Catherine Clément's *Opera, or The Undoing of Women*, notes with accuracy that Clément's writing "seems to owe little to standard academic procedure: it more closely resembles the web spun by a first-rate storyteller, the free-association ramblings of a subject on the psychoanalytic couch, a piece of music" (Clément x). Many readers like both stories and music, though they may prefer to enjoy them separately, and probably few would go out of their way to mix these forms of expression with the "free-association ramblings" of a psychoanalytic patient. Still, we live in crowded times, so it is not surprising to find even relatively conservative theoretical studies going off in two directions at once, as E. Ann Kaplan's does.

Kaplan's *Motherhood and Representation* (1992) is really two books. The first is a succinct though fairly complete and largely successful attempt at a unified field theory of semiotics, psychoanalytic theory, feminist theory, and cultural studies generally. This first "book" is ambitious and hopeful, whereas the second, smaller study, which deals with the specific subject described in Kaplan's subtitle, is unfinished and, if not pessimistic, at least somewhat wistful in tone.

Obviously there is a lot of room for overlap here, and, in fact, Kaplan's two "books" begin as one, with an analysis of three mothers: the historical mother, who is socially constructed ("the mother that girls are socialized to become" [6]); the psychoanalytic mother, who is articulated by Freud and later analysts and who dwells in the unconscious; and the fictional mother, the mother of films and novels, who is a combination of the historical and the psychoanalytic. In her preface, Kaplan hints at a fourth mother when she alludes briefly to her own experiences. I would call this one the personal mother and I regret not hearing more from her.

Kaplan points to three "eruptions" (17) that contribute to the construction of the historical mother as we know her today. The first of these economic, political, and technological convulsions is the Industrial Revolution, which turned the wife/mother from blue-collar producer in a communal setting to middle-class consumer and center of the nuclear family.

This early-modern mother, as Kaplan calls her, becomes the high-modern mother during World War I, or the second eruption. The nuclear family is now threatened by a variety of trends: women's return to the work force, the suffrage movement, the large number of women entering higher education or remaining childless or choosing lesbian relationships. The mother's position in the nuclear family is still central, though it is now a defensive position.

With the third eruption, World War II, the role of the traditional mother changes significantly, as does that of the other family members in the nuclear configuration: Mom goes to work, Dad does at least some of the nurturing, and the kids learn how to make their own snacks. When the house is quiet and the bedroom door is closed, what goes on between wife and husband is shaped by new attitudes and procedures, and the woman can delay, prevent, or accelerate both orgasm and conception. As of this writing, in fact, she can now exercise a prerogative heretofore available only to men and become a parent in old age, using her pension payments, if she chooses, not for dance lessons and cruise vacations but for diapers and baby food.

Initially, it is this historical mother whom Freud scrutinizes as part of his attempt to describe a formation, vast and inexorable, that he perceived as underlying ordinary human consciousness. To Freudians, the Oedipal conflict is the key to one's social construction, and those who handle the conflict successfully will be well-adjusted and productive, while those who do not can anticipate unhappy relationships and destructiveness. This "humanist/sociological" (28) view is based on parent-child interactions, and, while it is important to Kaplan, she gives greater emphasis to Lacanian theories that stress, not historical construction of social roles, but construction via linguistic and cultural systems. We may say that Lacan expands Freud's ideas horizontally, giving more attention at one end of the developmental period to the child's pre-Oedipal or "imaginary" life, where pleasure takes the form of a fusional bodily ecstasy called *jouissance,* and, at the other end, to the child's entrance into the "symbolic" sphere where his or her sexuality is constructed by language and culture.

Other theorists modify Lacan's teaching, and Kaplan emphasizes the writings of Luce Irigaray, who suggests that women can avoid the oppressive codes of the symbolic by using the language of the body; Hélène Cixous, whose ideas are similar to Irigaray's yet who emphasizes voice over touch; and Julia Kristeva, who implies (to Kaplan's demurral) that men achieve *jouissance* through language, women through biology—specifically, childbirth. Since consciously experienced language and culture are more malleable than unconscious experiences, Kaplan sees Lacan, Irigaray, and Kristeva as more optimistic than the humanist/sociological (read: deterministic) Freudians.

Yet Kaplan objects to a too-narrow focus not only by Lacan but also, by extension, by those who work within his paradigm. As she sees it, Lacan and the Lacanians emphasize the linguistic phenomena of the symbolic at the expense of what she calls the "here-and-now" (51) bonding of mother and child. To Kaplan, Lacan's "imaginary," "symbolic," and "real" (where deaths, wars, and natural disasters occur) are givens, but she does not see the phenomena of the imaginary as obscure and beyond understanding. In this view she is supported by David Stern, whose writings on early childhood argue for a mutuality between mother and child, even an agency on the child's part. Whereas Freud and Lacan would argue that an adult seized by erotic fantasies toward others is reliving an unconscious memory of oneness with the mother, Stern would say that the mutuality one practiced as a child with one's mother may now be practiced in an open and healthy manner with other adults. The actions described in each model are not so different, but Stern's outlook is more optimistic than Freud's and even Lacan's because of his emphasis on agency, that is, on the possibility for change.

Good, because the way mothers are portrayed in the twentieth century, they are going to need all the possibilities for change they can get. In the second part of her book—the second "book," really—Kaplan examines fictional mothers in *Now, Voyager,* as well as in *East Lynne, Marnie,* and other films. What she finds again and again is a kind of slippage from a purported examination of the historical mother to an unconscious treatment of the psychoanalytic mother. That is, the filmmakers, prompted by some social anxiety (over mothers entering the work force in large numbers, for example), make a film that is ostensibly about the socially constructed mother yet confuses her with the other, earlier mother, toward whom an unconscious hostility is projected. Kaplan finds that "realistic and non-paranoid mother images" appear only at times when women are making "few explicit or public demands" and that we see "how quickly paranoid representations return once women begin to articulate their oppressions" (179).

If readers find Kaplan's second "book" less interesting than the one that explicates and unifies different schools of critical theory, the fault lies in the examples used to bolster the argument rather than in the argument itself. Indeed, this is a generic difficulty: examples, especially ones examined in meticulous detail, as is the case here, are almost always less interesting than the arguments they support. In this instance, one needs to bear in mind that most films are made by only a handful of people and most are neither commercially nor critically successful. Thus it is hard to be convincing about the relevance of a small sample of films to a sweeping argument about social attitudes.

In fact, it is only in the last chapter that the second "book" really redeems itself, for here Kaplan uses numerous and varied examples from all sorts of media to support her thesis and not simply a few films. Here she discusses the cultural paradigm shift known as postmodernism, drawing on the writings of Jean Baudrillard, Frederic Jameson, and Jean-François Lyotard. Whereas the first three phases of historical motherhood occur in the machine-age phase of the Industrial Revolution, Kaplan sees a fourth phase occurring as the machine age becomes the electronic age. According to Baudrillard and the others, postmodernism means "the blurring of hitherto sacrosanct boundaries and polarities" as well as "the elimination of any position from which to speak or judge" and "the reduction of all to one level, often termed that of the simulacra" (181). Kaplan is entirely convincing here because she uses a variety of supportive examples, each of which is treated succinctly, to show how the simulacrum has come to dominate postmodern motherhood.

Two especially memorable examples are a televised "Mother-Daughter Pageant," a sort of cross-generational beauty pageant in which dress-alike pairs unconsciously (and grotesquely) parody true mother-daughter bonding, and *Video Baby*, the latest in a series of tapes that includes *Video Cat* and *Video Dog*. Kaplan quotes a *Wall Street Journal* article, which says that *Video Baby* makes it possible for people who don't have time to create families of their own to enjoy "the full, rich experience of parenthood without the mess and inconvenience of the real thing" (201). Without "the mess and inconvenience of the real thing," of course, there would be no artists to create, no audiences to appreciate their creations, and no theorists to study creators, creations, consumers, or other theorists.

Gender, Language, and Myth (1992), edited by Glenwood Irons, covers many of the same areas as *Motherhood and Representation*. Since it is a collection of essays, there is no single thesis, though clearly this book is a response to the sort of question Kaplan poses, namely, where does art come from? Some of the answers are the same, too: just as Kaplan links certain representations of motherhood to corresponding social changes, so, for example, does Jane Tompkins trace the rise of the western to "women's invasion of the public sphere between 1880 and 1920," believing it to be "no accident that men gravitated in imagination toward a womanless milieu, a set of rituals featuring physical combat and physical endurance, a mise-en-scène that, when it did not reject culture itself, prominently featured whiskey, gambling, and prostitution—three main targets of women's reform in the later years of the nineteenth century" (121).

In one way or another, each of these essays looks at genre fiction—the western but also romance, horror, science fiction, detective and spy novels, and films. As Umberto Eco observes, one crucial (and theoretically enticing) requirement of genre writing is that the writer must create, "not the Unknown, but the Already Known." Thus reading an Ian Fleming novel, says Eco, is like watching the Harlem Globetrotters play your local team: since "we know with absolute confidence that the Globetrotters will win," then "the pleasure lies in watching the trained virtuosity with which they defer the final moment, with what ingenious deviations they reconfirm the foregone conclusion, with what trickeries they make rings round their opponents." Eco draws a similar conclusion about the James Bond series, though he tosses in a gratuitous sneer à la Q. D. Leavis when he says that "the novels of Fleming exploit in exemplary measure that element of foregone play which is typical of the escape machine geared for the entertainment of the masses" (166). What is missing here is that intellectuals are part of the masses, too, and that while readers who prefer Marie Corelli are unlikely to read Henry James, those who prefer James will also read Corelli nonetheless.

Yet Eco's point about audiences' love for the Already Known is not only valid but compelling. Is it true that, as Irigaray has suggested, "we live in a homosexual culture privileging the male, who can only function with others modelled on himself, others who are his mirror reflections" (Grosz 107)? There is something to this: anyone who has ever watched a couple in a video store has seen the woman propose one film after another, sometimes with a plaintive appeal to the higher authority of the admiring critic quoted on the jacket, only to have the man shake his head again and again as he waits for her to bring him the perfect movie, the one that he has seen repeatedly, even though the title is never the same, and whose subject is himself. Certainly this insistence on the simulacrum shapes the various genres, which become ritualized in half-conscious patterns that are neglected or defied at the writer's peril: returning to the western for a moment, John Cawelti notes that one must not increase the level, randomness, or ambiguity in "the relatively orderly rituals of violence characteristic of the traditional western," because "there is a kind of redemption . . . through violence when it is used appropriately by the heroic individual" (97). Put a few bullets in the right place and you've saved the culture; put a few more bullets in the wrong place and you get a massacre.

Kaplan's and Irons's authors agree, then, that popular artists respond both to unconscious psychological realities and to social change by creating ritualized artifacts, which mirror the anxieties and desires of the masses in a funhouse-explosion of competing simulacra. But even if it is true that we love the Already Known, one question still remains, and it is one that will keep theorists in business for as long as artists are creating, namely: what is it that we Already Know?

Freud may have answered that question long ago with his idea of the contrary, that is, an object or idea in which two opposites do not simply coexist but mutually interpenetrate each other so deeply that it is impossible to tell where one ends and the other begins. "Ideas which are contraries are by preference expressed in dreams [and works of art, he might have said] by one and the same element." For this reason, meanings proliferate rather than diminish: " 'No' seems not to exist so far as dreams [and art works] are concerned" (*On Dreams* 661). One such contrary is the romance of Scarlett O'Hara and Rhett Butler; in his contribution to *Gender, Language, and Myth*, Leslie Fiedler notes that many readers of *Gone with the Wind* assume that Rhett will one day return to Scarlett's arms, "though the single line they are likely to be able to quote from the book is the one Rhett speaks as he leaves her, presumably forever, 'Frankly, my dear, I don't give a damn' " (60).

Regardless of the social pressures that helped generate *Gone with the Wind,* it is clear that the contrary Scarlett, at once the irresistible femme fatale and the easily discarded reject, can only have come from the unconscious, which is where the light of understanding flickers and expires; we blow out that light ourselves when we affix the prefix "un-" to that other human quality that we are so proud of, that sets us apart from (indeed, above) the other animals.

This is why Harold Schechter, writing of Tobe Hooper's film *The Texas Chainsaw Massacre,* writes, "in a very real sense, the appeal of Hooper's movie—the fascination it exerts—is beyond rational comprehension" (248). It is why, Carol J. Clover observes, "the processes by which a certain image (but not another) filmed in a certain way (but not another) causes one person's (but not another's) pulse to race finally remain a mystery—not only to critics and theorists but even, to judge from interviews and the trial-and-error (and baldly imitative) quality of the films themselves, to the people who make the product" (256).

In an earlier essay, I quoted Georges Braque as saying the only thing that counts in art is the thing you can't explain. Braque's pronouncement may be seen as tinged with determinism, perhaps even pessimism, as though one has to stand helpless and with eyes averted before the all-powerful Mystery. However, there is a way to agree with his assertion without sinking into a morbid anti-intellectualism. After all, as we ask ourselves where art comes from, it is possible to go altogether too far in the other direction, that is, away from mystery and toward clarity and free will.

We have already seen that Kaplan endorses David Stern's belief in personal agency over the determinism that others see (not always correctly, I feel) in Freud's writings. And it is not uncommon for some theorists, especially those whose writings are politically based, to rank other theorists in terms of their advocacy of the possibility of agency. Here, for example, is Susan McClary (in her study *Feminine Endings*) on Foucault vs. Gramsci and Bakhtin:

> While they offer extraordinary insight into the political machinations of culture, Foucault's formulations often are somewhat pessimistic, for they rarely admit of [*sic*] the possibility of agency, resistance, or alternative models of pleasure. Here the models of political criticism developed by Antonio Gramsci or Mikhail Bakhtin can serve as empowering correctives, in that they recognize and focus on cultural contestation, counternarratives, and carnivalesque celebrations of the marginalized. They conceive of culture as the terrain in which competing versions of social reality fight it out, and thus they permit the study of the ideological dimensions of art while avoiding the determinism that too often renders such analyses reductive. (McClary 29)

Gramsci and Bakhtin may make for cheerier theory, but do their well-lit, clear-headed formulations cover the entire terrain—cannot Foucault's "archaeologies" provide valuable information about what prompts, thwarts, and complicates the struggle between competing versions of social reality?

Too much reason leads to a kind of unreason, after all: in her foreword to Clément's condemnation of opera, McClary calls opera "an art form of the past," apparently not noticing that new ones are being written every day (Clément xvi). And though McClary maintains that Clément loves opera, the book ends with Clément's self-indulgent description of her dream of a New Age "pagan" festival that takes place in a world where "opera will no longer exist" (Clément 177). Free-association ramblings of a subject on the psychoanalytic couch, indeed: McClary's and Clément's pronouncements against opera are set out with a clarity as brutal as that which informs Leavis's censure of movies and best-sellers. If we abolish both operas and soap operas, then the art world will be severely truncated at both ends, and a cold, inhuman lucidity will dominate what remains.

When I encounter calls for more representations of personal agency in art, I am uncomfortably reminded of a desire on the part of certain naive students that the novels I assign them be about affable, good-natured, sure-to-succeed sorts instead of the outcast adulteresses, runaway slaves, and other marginal types who figure largely in the pages of fiction. But part of art and, if not the largest part, at least the most important part—"the thing you can't explain"—comes from the unconscious. The unconscious gives birth to those contraries that, more often than not, lead not to corporation presidencies and happy, stable marriages, as the naive students want, but to tragedy.

Comedy may be easier to take, and, personally, I would rather watch a performance of *As You Like It* than one of *Macbeth*. Still, tragedy is the most resonant of the genres: in one of the best books on the creative process, Albert Rothenberg writes, "Literary tragedies arise from . . . antithetical elements, such as freedom in slavery, pride in humility, or triumph in defeat. When these antithetical qualities are revealed or elaborated as a tragic novel or play unfolds, there is always an element of surprise, the culmination and overall impact of the suspenseful journey the creator has given us" (232). It is hard to think of reading a book or watching a movie or play that contains no element of surprise. Even when we are dealing with the Already Known, we will be disappointed unless we stumble unexpectedly across what we Already Know.

These last paragraphs should not be taken as an endorsement

of obscurantism. After all, we are talking about the smallest component of art here. "The thing you can't explain," while crucial to an art work, is in the same proportion to the rest of the work as the spoonful of yeast is to the cupfuls of flour, water, and so on that combine to make a loaf of bread. Theory measures everything that it can, which is almost everything; the unconscious provides the rest.

Reviewers in the Popular Press
and Their Impact on the Novel

For a book to receive any sort of review at all, it seems, is something of a miracle. The Women in Publishing group in England reports that over fifty thousand books are published in Great Britain yearly, yet the *Times Literary Supplement* has the space to review only about three thousand, or around 6 percent. Books reviewed in *TLS* are likely to be sufficiently high-profile to be covered multiply in other, less prestigious organs, further limiting the total number of titles covered.

Suppose, however, that as many as two thousand more books are reviewed in media from specialty journals to small-town newspapers. Even then, a new book has only a one in ten chance of being reviewed even once and no more than a fifty-fifty chance of being reviewed positively. Novelists whose books are reviewed negatively are likely to wish their work had been ignored; at least they must ask themselves, who reviews these books anyway?

Two related questions are, do reviews affect the writing and publishing of novels, and, if so, in what ways? There is, as it turns out, a symbiotic relationship between the novel and the critical review, both of which came into being at approximately the same time and matured at roughly the same pace. A look at the historical record shows that indeed reviews do have an impact on writing and publishing, though that impact is probably less than many think. A corollary is that, if reviewers affect novelists to some degree, so novelists improve reviewing standards by broadening reviewers' horizons.

First, the matter of who writes reviews. Though there are societies for reviewers such as the National Book Critics Circle in the United States, there are no associations to enforce standards comparable to the American Medical Association and the American Bar Association and certainly no procedures established for the certification or even the training of reviewers. Indeed, the first reviewers scarcely reviewed at all: J. M. S. Tompkins reveals that the typical eighteenth-century English reviewer preferred lengthy quotation of the novel in hand to critical commentary, often quoting as many as a dozen pages and further lightening his work load by taking them from the book's first chapters only. Bad novels were dismissed briefly and witheringly; good ones were praised at slightly greater length for such dubious qualities as decency, plausibility, and freedom from affectation.

But if early reviewing practices were so slipshod and even lazy, surely part of the reason for this lack of professionalism can be traced to the equivocal state of the novel itself. After all, if measured by present-day standards, the first novels often seem unworthy of the name. Looking back at seventeenth-century France, when the first full-length books of prose fiction began to appear with some frequency in that country, Martin Turnell notes that "the writers were not without talent but their works, as we can see from the practice of Honoré d'Urfé and Madeleine de Scudéry, often consisted of lengthy collections of adventure and love stories which today are found unreadable and a serious burden for literary historians. The plot was used to introduce and link them together, but there were no compelling relations between them or with the main plot, which meant that the novel was usually lacking in a unified experience." No wonder reviewers found themselves stymied in the face of such an ungainly form.

The task of early reviewers was further complicated by the early novel's aura of disreputability. Each new medium is viewed suspiciously in contrast to the old, and, just as new forms of pop music or electronic media are seen today as threats to established values, so the novel was seen as an inferior alternative to the poem, with the novel itself being seen as a bastardization of the romance, whereas the romance was already a step down from the epic. As late as 1828, a writer for the English *Athenaeum* maintained that a reader whose intellectual faculties are at their peak will pick up a poem, though when fatigued we are more likely to "court embicility [*sic*] and inanition in the pages of a novel." An anonymous colleague writing in the *Methodist Magazine* suggested rhetorically that readers "ask the man, who with smiling but vacant countenance, rises from reading *Tom Jones, Don Quixote*, etc., if his judgment is better informed; if his mind is more expanded; his stock of ideas increased; or if he is better prepared for performing the duties of his station?"

The answer, of course, is no. Yet even if this smiling, vacant reader finds himself unable to adequately perform his duties as merchant or barrister or clergyman because of the novel's pernicious influence on his intellect and sense of purpose, his continued interest in and support of the novel as literary commodity has now become absolutely essential. For two events occurring in the last half of the eighteenth century combined to change forever the nature of publishing: the birth of the novel, which would rapidly become the popular form it remains today; and the death of the patronage system, which meant that writers would have to be supported in their industry by thousands of individual purchasers of their books instead of a single wealthy nobleman. And these two developments led to a third: the installation of the reviewer at midpoint between the writer and the book-buying public.

Frank Donoghue sees in the career of Laurence Sterne the emblematic story of the first modern novelist. At the beginning of his career, Sterne, like other authors of his day, believed that reliance on a wealthy and noble patron was the only road to publication.

He struck out on his own, however, when he decided to promote the sales of *Tristram Shandy* (1759–67) with the help of David Garrick, actor, theater manager, and, perhaps most important, influential member of fashionable London society. Wildly successful, *Tristram Shandy* spawned an immense amount of "Sterneiana"— imitations of and pamphlets about the novel. When these fell off in number, Sterne found his work treated in two of the most influential of the new journals devoted to reviewing, the *Monthly Review* (1749) and the *Critical Review* (1755).

Far from praising Sterne's work, though, as had the amateurish yet enthusiastic imitators and pamphleteers, writers for the two literary reviews insisted that he abandon the learned satire of *Tristram Shandy* and take on instead the familiar world of feeling. The result is the very different *A Sentimental Journey* (1767), based on Sterne's own travels in France and Italy. Within less than a decade, then, Sterne not only went from dependence to self-promotion to reliance on reviews but also changed his way of writing in order to accommodate critical opinion.

If Sterne's relations with the critical reviewers were not entirely happy, at least his work was taken seriously by them. Women novelists of the day found their work regarded uniformly as second-rate; male reviewers condescended to female novelists, though they spared them the withering scorn that was the lot of inferior male novelists. Women writers resorted to various strategies to win critical approval, seeking endorsements from male literary sponsors, for example, or addressing exclusively female audiences in the hopes of avoiding the charge of meddling in serious (i.e., masculine) affairs.

Fanny Burney, however, took the matter directly in hand by dedicating her first novel, *Evelina* (1778), to the "Authors of the *Monthly* and *Critical Review*," reminding the critics of the principles they themselves had defined in their own pages (integrity, candor, and so on) and arguing how *Evelina* satisfied every one of their criteria. The immediate effect of this bold stroke was slight, since *Evelina* received polite but perfunctory notices in both reviews. But both reviews praised extensively her next novel, *Cecilia* (1782). Thus Burney's initiative and its effect make her, as Donoghue says, the first author to acknowledge openly and seriously that critical reviews "occupy a legitimate place of power in the field of literature." (Not that the reviewers took women as a whole any more seriously; a century later, a reviewer said of George Eliot's work, "There is a good deal of coarseness, which it is unpleasant to think of as the work of a woman." Yet when Eliot was believed to be a man by reviewers, she was thought to be "a gentleman of high church tendencies.")

For the fact is that, in general, if most reviewers throughout history have proven to be more open to novelty and variety in fiction than most readers, they have also shown themselves to be more conservative than most literary (as opposed to mass-market) novelists. Henry Nash Smith points out that, in the United States, Hawthorne, Melville, and James all started out successfully but suffered drastic declines in sales in midcareer; William Dean Howells could not break from the hackneyed convention of the genteel love story, even though his own tastes were shaped by the achievements of the groundbreaking English, French, and Russian novelists of his day; and Twain was treated as little more than a comedian by reviewers who failed to notice the thematic depth of his work.

Part of the problem, of course, was that these authors opposed what Herbert F. Smith calls "the Protestant ethic of the American heartland of the mid–nineteenth century . . . based upon the triumvirate of values that support it still: success, reform, and piety." For example, in his novels Hawthorne explored ancestral guilt, a topic of little interest to the reader whose self-concept was based on the fundamental American premise of rebirth and renewal in a New World. Not surprisingly, the reviewer for a magazine called *To-Day* found *The Scarlet Letter* (1850) "gloomy from beginning to end," and other reviewers found both "pollution" and "mentally diseased" ideas in *The Scarlet Letter* and *The Blithedale Romance* (1852).

And after delighting audiences with early novels based on his real-life travels in the South Pacific and then baffling them with the more demanding *Mardi* (1849) and *Moby-Dick* (1851), the always-unpredictable Melville tried to resolve the conflict between audience demand and artistic desire with *Pierre* (1852), one of the most bizarre works in U.S. or any literature. As Henry Nash Smith writes, the plan was "to produce a novel that on the surface would conform to the conventions of mass fiction as these were represented in weekly 'story papers,' yet would embody an undercurrent of subversive implication repudiating the basic articles of the dominant value system." Melville hoped he could accomplish two goals at once: win back his readership with, on the surface, the kind of sentimental pulp fiction that was devoured unthinkingly by the masses, yet gain the admiration of the few elite readers capable of responding to true genius by including a second, subtler layer of thought that could be detected only by the cognoscenti.

The result is that *Pierre* is a bizarre hybrid, something vaguely reminiscent of the romances Charles Brockden Brown had written half a century before, long before Hawthorne had perfected the American form of that genre in *The Scarlet Letter,* yet freighted, especially in the final chapters, with personal grousings. An aristocratic country youth in the beginning, Pierre is revealed as a writer and misunderstood genius (much like his creator) halfway through; by the end he is a killer, a prisoner, and, finally, a suicide.

Some happy ending! Reviewers were not pleased—even Melville's friend Evert Duyckinck, writing in the *Literary World,* condemned Pierre's inconsistencies and overreachings, observing that "the combined power of New England transcendentalism and Spanish Jesuitical casuistry could not have more completely befogged nature and truth, than this confounded Pierre has done." Others were more direct: following the publication of *Pierre,* one New York newspaper ran the headline, "HERMAN MELVILLE

CRAZY." Whereas conservative reviewers persuaded Laurence
Sterne to be less experimental in his writing and more conciliatory
to a mass audience, the literary press was as violent to Melville's
outlook as he to theirs; in effect, devastating notices killed the public's desire for his writings altogether.

It should be noted, however, that reviewers' opinions are not always so influential and that the reviewing system is only part of a
vast industry whose output is shaped by a variety of factors, some
of which lie beyond anyone's control. For example, there is nothing
more relentless (and less predictable) than literary fashion: as H. R.
Klienberger points out, after the German translation of *Robinson
Crusoe* (1719) was published in 1720, twenty imitations of it appeared in German over the next ten years and several more in the
following decade; in effect, this story of self-reliance and Christian
piety had created its own self-renewing publicity machine.

In the same way, a work adored by professional readers is doomed
to a respectful neglect if lay readers do not embrace it. Christoph
Martin Wieland's *History of Agathon* (1765–66), though it initiated the tradition of the Bildungsroman or educational novel, "was
to share the fate of many outstanding contributions to German
fiction," says Klienberger: "It was acclaimed by creative writers
and critics, but not widely read." A later Bildungsroman, Goethe's
Wilhelm Meister's Apprenticeship (1795–96), is probably the first
example of the genre that comes to the minds of most readers, but
probably less because of expert opinion than the fact that it, too
(like *Robinson Crusoe*), was widely read and imitated not only in
its country of origin but internationally.

So reviewers do not affect sales of novels perhaps as much as
they would like to. Obviously, best-sellers like Judith Krantz and
Danielle Steel sell very well at present, even though they are reviewed very rarely and, even then, usually negatively. On the other
hand, reviewers are able to shape the production of serious novelists, as the examples of Sterne and Melville show. And, of course,

serious novelists who do not discourage easily are able to change reviewers' minds as well; as we have seen, Fanny Burney's dedication of her first book to reviewers may have influenced their overwhelming acceptance of her second. And Henry Nash Smith points out that, whereas James's *Portrait of a Lady* (1881) was accused of being overly analytical by reviewers and *The Bostonians* (1886) and *The Princess Casamassima* (1886) were called "heartless," a change of tone began to appear in reviews of *The Spoils of Poynton* (1897) and *What Maisie Knew* (1897) as critics began to write more positively of the subtlety and refinement of James's method.

As noted earlier, to the extent that they are influential at all, reviewers are somewhat supportive of the public's fairly conservative taste in reading, although, as a group, they are more willing to accept new developments in writing; thus reviewers help general readers to change their literary attitudes, though probably not as quickly as the novelists themselves would like. The Women in Publishing group asked literary editors what sorts of books they selected for reviewing; such answers as "fairly widely available, reasonably cheap, not too academic" and "academic with a small 'a' " suggest that the books most likely to be reviewed will be serious yet accessible, books that fall into the midrange somewhere between potboilers and scholarship.

In a recent survey of some twenty regional U.S. newspapers, Robert Johnson found that reviewers are considerably more professional than they were in the eighteenth century. "Writing styles . . . seemed carefully weighed," with "little, if any, bombast, let alone fluff. Comfortably colloquial, but formal, diction and sentence patterns dominated," even if "highly educated diction appeared to be on holiday." Overall, Johnson found popular reviewing in this country to be serious, if not stuffy, a matter of "avowed book people talking to other book people . . . not the odd tourist who got lost while paging through on the way to NBA scores."

No doubt many novelists feel that reviewers are not sufficiently respectful of their best efforts. However, an astute writer will offer change gradually rather than ask the reading public to alter its habits overnight. In this sense, a tolerant if skeptical reviewer may serve a function somewhat like that of a sea anchor, keeping the boat from lurching forward so quickly that the passengers fall off. In the complex calculus whose variables include reader, writer, critic, and book, each element is essential.

M. L. Rosenthal and Our Life in Poetry

As a rule, book reviewers do not occupy the most exalted position within the literary community. According to Shelley, "reviewers, with some rare exceptions, are a most stupid and malignant race." And Shelley was not alone in thinking that the average reviewer probably doesn't deserve to die a natural death.

One would like to think, however, that Shelley would have classed M. L. Rosenthal among his "rare exceptions." In *Our Life in Poetry*, Rosenthal comes across as a writer of uncommon care, subtlety, and erudition. Yet his point of departure is a simple one; thinking over his long career as a reviewer for *Poetry*, the *Nation*, the *New York Times*, and others, Rosenthal reflects that his basic critical approach is "to try to grasp what I see and hear in a poem, just by opening myself to it as best I can."

The result is criticism that is not only sonorous and discerning but also merits a permanence rarely accorded this type of writing. Rosenthal is epigrammatic in a way that is provocative yet perceptive. Thus E. E. Cummings is a poet whom "no one really hates . . . for the coy prettiness of some of his posturing," though reading his collected poems is "like eating a whole cheesecake at one sitting." Kathleen Raine's "pain . . . stays mainly in the brain." The impoverished and self-effacing Kenneth Fearing is "America's one adult poet-in-a-garret." Dylan Thomas, "who had the air of a precocious baby, actually was one." And there were two Robert Frosts: "the first, truest Robert Frost has the gloom of a great Russian writer," but the second is merely a "smiling public man."

One of the most helpful techniques a reviewer can use to introduce an unfamiliar writer or give new significance to a familiar one is the startlingly apt comparison, in which the reviewer rubs two writers together to produce unexpected sparks. Rosenthal is particularly masterful here, as when he calls Auden a twentieth-century Dryden or says that an original and audacious figure like Wallace Stevens forces such younger poets as Richard Wilbur to be blander and more discursive.

On rare occasion, Rosenthal goes comparison-crazy, as when he associates Allen Ginsberg with Patchen, Céline, Whitman, Williams, and Fearing—but then he redeems himself with the most apt comparison of all, to George Metesky, the so-called "Mad Bomber" who kept New Yorkers on edge in the fifties with his homemade explosives. After all, in *Howl*, Ginsberg "hurls, not only curses, but *everything*."

The prizewinner in the comparison department is the description of Wallace Stevens, clearly one of Rosenthal's favorites, as "a tall, overweight Keats with normal temperature and an important position in an insurance firm." (He makes another sort of comparison altogether when, describing Stevens's walled-in sensibility and acceptance of outward life while keeping his own inward life intact, Rosenthal alludes to the Maine man whose epitaph reads, "He et what was sot before him.")

But how many book reviews can a reader read in a single sitting? After all, the individual pieces that make up *Our Life in Poetry* were meant to be read singly over a period of years. One ploy Rosenthal uses to keep the reader reading is the impossible-to-ignore first sentence, the kind that immediately produces its own echo. Thus, "what is American poetry today?" (right, what *is* it?). Or "how shall we think of Charles Olson's poetry?" (yes, how *shall* we?). There is often a coy negative in these first sentences, as when he decries "the way William Carlos Williams is being published in England" (say, what *are* those Britishers doing to our boy?) or confesses that he "never knew Delmore Schwartz intimately" (then how well *did* he know him?) or laments that "Dilys Lang was not famous" (why *not*, for heaven's sake?).

Then, once brought into the review by the come-hither quality of the first sentence, one is kept there by Rosenthal's capacity for the telling epigram. His specialty is loading much information into few words, as in this one-sentence assessment of the great moderns: "William Butler Yeats remains our greatest modern poet, Ezra Pound our great embroiler and William Carlos Williams our great humanizer, but Eliot, while he was still enmeshed in unresolved youthful struggles of spirit, showed us a decisive image of ourselves in the mirror of a terrified age being quick-marched nowhere though still capable of making wonderful jokes about it." Rosenthal uses labels like "great" and "greatest" more frequently than some readers might like, but, as he himself says about his use of the tag "Jewish poetry," a label is best employed "if one does not press too hard" and is "more useful for inviting empathy with subtle, elusive processes than for establishing categories."

Something else that makes these reviews valuable is what might be called their prophetic value. To give a single instance: writing of Randall Jarrell, clearly not one of his favorites, Rosenthal wonders "whether a New Sentimentality is not arising, even more deadly than that of the nineteenth century because clad in the technical efficiency which is our dazzling legacy from Pound and Eliot." This was written in 1948; in the February 1991 issue of *Poetry,* William Logan laments the absence of wit in American poetry and the fact that "American poetry is more troubled with sentiment" than leavened with humor. Assuming Logan is right—and I think he is—then Rosenthal's prediction of a largely humorless and sentimental American poetry has been borne out more than forty years later.

A student of contemporary poetry could do worse than to read

Our Life in Poetry in tandem with the *Norton Anthology of Modern Poetry* and let Rosenthal lead the way, turning up the light here, pointing out the unseen there, and confirming, to paraphrase another epigrammatist, what one has known all along but never said quite so well.

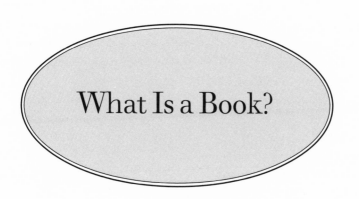

What Is a Book?

Ghosts and Gadabouts

GOTHIC AND PICARESQUE
IN THE AMERICAN NOVEL

The American novel, in all its variety, does not reflect American life so much as it refracts it, concentrating the diffuse light of daily existence into the concentrated radiance of art. From the beginning, the American novel reveals a sense of personal displacement that is presented more as a fact of life in the New World than as a misfortune. If you read the headlines, you know that not very many of us out there seem to feel at home in our own skin. And to a large extent, this idea of displacement still characterizes American fiction today.

The English settlers who came to seventeenth-century America left behind one concept of identity and, upon arriving, put another in its place. In the London they left, the household of a typical tradesman might consist of a dozen or more persons: father, mother, children, journeymen, apprentices, servants. This basic social unit was no more secure than any that succeeded it, yet the insecurity of the individual members was different from that of their successors. Each adult and child was rooted in a locale and in a family pattern that had changed little, if at all, from what it had been before and what it would be in the next generation, and thus each person knew his or her fixed place both within and outside of the household.

Economic and social upheaval in the Old World changed forever the essentially feudal lot of the tradesman and his family, of course, but while this traditional pattern is still an important part of the English national memory, in America it never existed at all. America may be the land of the free, but democracy exacts a price for the freedom it confers. New systems of politics, economics, science, technology: these intoxicating changes also left the individual reeling under the effect of forces that seemed beyond his control. Is it any wonder that the first American novels deal with displacement, even terror?

The June 1798 issue of the Philadelphia *Weekly Magazine* contained a "Recipe for a Modern Romance" that poked fun at the Gothic fiction tradition while, like all satires, it reminded readers of the importance of the object of its comic intentions. Perfected in England by such writers as Horace Walpole and Mrs. Radcliffe, the Gothic tale, macabre, fantastic, and supernatural, was set customarily in graveyards, ruins, and wild landscapes. Indeed, the *Weekly Magazine* invited would-be Gothic writers to take a haunted castle, partially destroy it, people it with aged servants, and send there a young lady who, after seeing skeletons, ghosts, and other apparitions, will be rescued by a handsome lover, whom she will then marry.

Except for the tidy conclusion, the essential ingredients of this "recipe," refined and embellished, are used again and again in major American novels, from Charles Brockden Brown's *Wieland* (1798) to Henry James's *The Turn of the Screw* (1898). Even in the all-male worlds of Poe's *Narrative of Arthur Gordon Pym of Nantucket* (1838) and Melville's *Moby-Dick* (1851), phantoms, ghosts, and creatures from the underworld spring from below-decks and appear on the masts of the huge creaking ships that, in American fiction, replace the European castles with their dungeons and towers.

The political founders of America, men like Thomas Jefferson, Benjamin Franklin, and John and Samuel Adams, were followers of Locke and other Enlightenment figures and thought humankind capable of tolerance, democracy, and reason. They were right, of course, if only partially so. The Gothic mindset accounts for everything the Enlightenment overlooks: terror, perversity, strangeness, a sense of not knowing where one is or how one got there. It is a way of viewing the world that continues to affect American fiction and that appears in works by such twentieth-century authors as William Faulkner, Flannery O'Connor, Ralph Ellison, Truman Capote, Thomas Berger, and Joyce Carol Oates.

A second strong current in the growing tide of early American literary thinking is the picaresque. The picaro, as seen in novels by writers like Daniel Defoe and Tobias Smollett, is a person of low birth, no particular occupation, and flexible morals. Typically a young man of dubious or unknown parentage, the picaro is pitchforked into the world at an early age and must make his way however he can. His story is a broadly appealing one, since most readers have to do things they dislike, even though they retain an essentially positive self-image, and since most expect to be knocked about and yet prosper in the end. Hence, despite considerable controversy, the enduring popularity of the premier American picaro, Huckleberry Finn, as well as such kindred as Melville's seafaring narrators and the protagonists of novels as varied as Stephen Crane's *The Red Badge of Courage* (1895), J. D. Salinger's *The Catcher in the Rye* (1951), and Russell Banks's *Rule of the Bone* (1995).

In many novels, early and late, both Gothic and picaresque elements figure, connoting the extremes of enclosure and mobility that often seem the only choices for protagonists whose home lives are haunted yet whose prospects on the open road are menaced by the unknown. Like Gothicism, the picaresque is a European import, and though both influences immediately take on American characteristics, together they show the enduring power of cultural artifacts. Leaving behind one's social and economic life is one thing, but the products of one's culture are not so easily abandoned.

In the uncertain world of the young nation, American authors often favored the romance, with its greater tolerance for authorial fancy, over the more literal novel. Gothic and picaresque elements abound, and characters are sustained by their own self-questioning, believing, often rightly, that the self will find no home in such a world. The English poet Stephen Spender observed once that whereas English writers are self-actualizers, heirs to modes of vision so venerable as to seem impersonal and absolute, American writers are self-creators who always seem to be rubbing their eyes in disbelief and uncertainty. For this reason, perhaps, characters in nineteenth-century American fiction often appear to lack confidence in what they should do and be.

In English fiction of this period, works often conclude with marriage, an act that legitimizes sexual relationships, affirms selfhood, and expresses a faith in a future peopled by the children that will result. In American fiction, by contrast, marriage is either out of the question or doomed, as if to say that a future is not possible. Leslie Fiedler points out how many classic American authors depict pairs of male characters, one light-skinned and one dark, who elude women, marriage, and community by fleeing into the wilderness together. Early examples include Cooper's Natty Bumppo and Chingachgook, Melville's Ishmael and Queequeg, and Twain's Huck and Jim, pairings that foreshadow the characterization in such later novels as Ken Kesey's *One Flew Over the Cuckoo's Nest* (1962).

When communities do form, often they are foredoomed. Hawthorne's *Blithedale Romance* (1852) is the chronicle of a utopian community that splinters into a mockery of the ideals it hoped to attain. Where there is closure in fiction of this period, it is often outside of the story proper, as at the end of *The Scarlet Letter* (1850), when the elf-child Pearl is exorcised of New World ghosts only after she flees to Europe. Similarly, the black family that suffers so in Harriet Beecher Stowe's *Uncle Tom's Cabin* (1852) must go to Africa to find peace.

This is not to say that these works are pessimistic or cynical about the individual's prospects in America. Rather, they recognize the ambivalent standing of the individual in an unformed culture and, on occasion, even acknowledge opportunities for progress. For example, Hester Prynne may not learn from her scarlet letter the lesson that the Puritans intend, yet Hawthorne goes to great length to describe how, in her isolation from the community, she develops powers of speculation that permit her to predict that, "at some brighter period, when the world should have grown ripe for it . . . a new truth would be revealed, in order to establish the whole relation between man and woman on a surer ground of mutual happiness." There is no progress without violence, and many antebellum works seem bent on clearing away the vestiges of destructive European thinking that have survived the Atlantic crossing.

In the aftermath of the Civil War, the novel per se, with its emphasis on realism and believability, becomes the dominant form for long fiction. This was a time of territorial expansion (Alaska was purchased in 1867), of new resources (the Nevada silver rush occurred in 1873), of new inventions (the telephone in 1876, the light bulb in 1879), and new industries (the Union Pacific railroad was completed in 1869, and a year later the Standard Oil Corporation was founded).

This is arguably the most energetic period in the life of the American novel, with book after book reflecting the burgeoning on every front of American life. Before the Civil War, novelists had no reason to suspect the power of human forces yet to come; after World War I, novelists either railed against the monsters of technology and capitalism or gave in to them. In his novelistic autobiography *The Education of Henry Adams* (1907), Adams describes himself as lying on the floor before a dynamo at the Great

Exposition of 1900, "his historical neck broken by the irruption of forces totally new." Even as refined an artist as Henry James is described by Ezra Pound as having a style that was like a huge engine capable of heaving the novelist out of himself, out of his personal limitations.

The literary realism that appeared in this period is best understood in the plural sense, one of a variety of schools. Mark Twain represents the high point of what we might call frontier realism, with its folksy humor and local color. His two Hannibal novels as well as works such as *Roughing It* (1872) show his realism to be the homely variety, a depiction of life at its most bumptious and uncouth. By contrast, Henry James is a pioneer in the field of psychological realism. His groundbreaking novel *The Portrait of a Lady* (1882), with its use of the "center of consciousness" technique, puts the reader within the protagonist's mind in order to ponder that character's thoughts about the action rather than the action itself. William Dean Howells was another type of American realist, one who adapted English realism for an American audience. Such works of his as *A Hazard of New Fortune* (1889) are American stories shot through with social concerns and observations on human nature of the kind associated with Dickens, Thackeray, and Trollope. The more refined realism of James and Howells is extended by Edith Wharton in such novels as *The Age of Innocence* (1920), in which characters who flout convention do so at their peril.

Like the earlier romances, few of the great realist novels end confidently, either, further evidence of the continuing sense of ambivalence felt by American characters as they alternate between stasis and flight. No novel illustrates this dilemma better than *The Adventures of Huckleberry Finn* (1885), where there seems no choice for the characters except the stifling confinement of "civilization" or the footloose life of the western wanderer. Other works of the period do actually posit faith in the idea of a sustaining common culture, including Sarah Orne Jewett's local-color novel *The Country of the Pointed Firs* (1896). Ironically, this same affirmative possibility, after much turmoil and pain, often marks the conclusion of the slave narrative, such as Harriet Jacobs's *Incidents in the Life of a Slave Girl* (1861), a form echoed in such twentieth-century works as Charles Johnson's *Oxherding Tale* (1982) and Toni Morrison's *Beloved* (1987).

As faith in political and religious institutions was eroded by a rising belief in science and such doctrines as Herbert Spencer's social Darwinism, literature responded with a narrowing of realism, with its promise of objectivity, into a more doctrinaire naturalism. Naturalism views the individual as confused, helpless, and victimized by social and economic factors beyond his control and understanding. Naturalistic novels include such works as Stephen Crane's *Maggie: A Girl of the Streets* (1893), Frank Norris's *McTeague* (1899), and Theodore Dreiser's *Sister Carrie* (1900).

The naturalistic trend continues in the twentieth century, though often in synthesis with the symbolism that shaped the poetry of the day: Ernest Hemingway's *The Sun Also Rises* (1926) is the tale of an ineffectual "lost generation," but Jake Barnes's emasculation is every bit as representative of the decline of the West as is the impotence of the Fisher King in T. S. Eliot's *The Waste Land* (1922). The essential American ingredients of uncertainty and dislocation that are embodied in the Gothic and picaresque traditions continue to be seen in such novels as Faulkner's *The Sound and the Fury* (1929) and *Light in August* (1932), works haunted by psychological rather than supernatural terrors, and F. Scott Fitzgerald's *The Great Gatsby* (1925) and *Tender Is the Night* (1934), with their rootless, amoral characters.

Yet if early American life is viewed tragically by novelists of the day, later life is more commonly seen as absurd by contemporary writers. This shift in mode is occasioned by a shift in the individual's view of himself in relation to the larger world. It would have been tragic, in the eighteenth or nineteenth century, to be struck by lightning, which might have seemed an act of God to survivors saddened yet comforted in their certainty that life has a divine purpose, however mysterious. By contrast, in more recent times it would be absurd rather than tragic to be killed by a terrorist's blast, because this would be a preventable act perpetrated by one human on another, and for no overarching reason.

Thus in works as different as Melville's *Benito Cereno* (1856), Hawthorne's *The Marble Faun* (1860), James's *Daisy Miller* (1879), and Twain's *A Connecticut Yankee in King Arthur's Court* (1889), individuals struggle against larger forces that overwhelm and eventually destroy them, as in classical tragedy. Yet in Faulkner's *Sanctuary* (1931), Djuna Barnes's *Nightwood* (1936), John Barth's *Giles Goat-Boy* (1966), and Thomas Pynchon's *The Crying of Lot 49* (1966), individuals challenge an indifferent or malevolent world and, when they prove unable to alter it, simply shrug, thereby acknowledging the absurdity of the situation, and go on with their lives.

Now that America has, with other developed nations, largely left the Industrial Age and entered the Age of Information, it remains to be seen how American novels will refract the events of a new way of living. Change is constant in American writing, and one needs only to look back over a brief period to see potentially significant trends already taking form. In the past few decades, for example, writers seem to be reflecting a widespread concern about personal identity by writing either memoir-like novels or a so-called "creative nonfiction" in which actual memoirs are given shape through fictive techniques. Novelists as different as Susan Cheever, Mary Gordon, William Styron, John Updike, Geoffrey Wolff, and Tobias Wolff explore old themes, yet they do so in ways that will only receive ample critical attention in years to come.

At the same time, fresh voices shaped by other cultures are transforming the American novel in exciting ways as authors such as

Maxine Hong Kingston, Amy Tan, Oscar Hijuelos, Thomas Sanchez, Julia Alvarez, and Cristina García enrich, alter, and, possibly,
even replace the traditional elements of American literary culture.

Yet it seems unlikely that the essential element of displacement
will disappear entirely. In an 1865 essay, Henry James warned that
Gothic terrors were no longer to be found in scary old castles but
in cheerful country estates. Can there be any doubt at present that
those same apparitions have multiplied and invaded our tract
houses and condominiums? Too, even though it is now possible to
explore every corner of the world at home via computer, it seems
doubtful that the picaresque tradition will be abandoned totally.
After all, according to John Gardner, author of *Grendel* (1971) and
other novels, there are only two plots: a stranger rides into town and
a stranger rides out of town. It seems likely that the novelists of to-
morrow will tell us that the ancient demons have not disappeared
but only changed form, that there is still reason to flee.

Born in the Marketplace

THE EMERGENCE OF THE AMERICAN NOVEL

To witness the death throes of antebellum American culture, a time traveler might visit Pfaff's restaurant-saloon on Broadway some evening in the 1850s. As American society became increasingly rigid and commercialized, the Bohemians at Pfaff's tried desperately to cling to the almost-childish innocence of simpler times, laughing and singing even as they watched their world come to an end. Here a visitor might see actresses, artists, comedians, poets, and novelists shouting to one another, telling jokes, drinking beer, puffing on cigars. The writers present might include Walt Whitman as well as Fitz-James O'Brien and Charles D. Gardette, two fictionists who patterned their work after Edgar Allan Poe's. Indeed, the recently deceased Poe, whose novel *The Narrative of Arthur Gordon Pym of Nantucket* (1838) describes a young man's flight from commerce and respectability, figured as a sort of patron saint for the merry cynics at Pfaff's.

Their forced gaiety and underlying gloom mirrors the emotions of Pym himself, who prefers the risk of starvation and cannibalism in the South Pacific to what he sees as the living death of the lawyer and businessman he will become if he stays in Nantucket. As Americans bid goodbye to a largely agrarian world, the Industrial Revolution moved into its maturity, with an attendant need for the increasingly complex and narrow roles played by workers-turned-specialists. In literature and the arts in general, now-familiar boundaries between high, middlebrow, and popular culture began to appear, becoming rigid after the Civil War. Earlier, Shakespeare was performed on the same stage as farces and minstrel shows; political rallies included poetry and musical performance; and popular songs were derived from operatic arias, just as classical compositions incorporated folk music. David S. Reynolds compares antebellum utopian life at Brook Farm, depicted in Nathaniel Hawthorne's *The Blithedale Romance* (1852), with the more hierarchical way of life described in Edward Bellamy's novel *Looking Backward* (1888). In the former, people live communally, enjoying poetry readings, concerts, and *tableaux vivants* along with their daily work, whereas in the latter, life is more rigidly ordered, with music piped into separate living compartments and much of the work done by machines.

A glance back and then forward, at the careers of two very different authors, reveals two very different Americas. In 1839, Herman Melville published his first professional work, "Fragments from a Writing Desk," in a newspaper in Lansingburgh, New York. He also shipped as a deckhand on the *St. Lawrence*, a medium-sized merchant vessel bound for Liverpool; later, he would base his novel *Redburn* (1849) on that trip. Once home, Melville was then employed as schoolteacher at the Greenbush Academy in Greenbush, New York. That a sailor whose own schooling had stopped at age fifteen could become a teacher—indeed, that one person could be author, sailor, and teacher in the same year—is a powerful reminder of the unsettled state of Melville's America and, in particular, of the laxity with which the professions were viewed.

By contrast, by the century's end, Henry James, a novelist as representative of that time as Melville was of his, reflected a changed view of the professions, including authorship, in his preface to *The Wings of the Dove* (1902), when he compares the novelist to a civil engineer who erects a bridge and then, as "rueful builder," passes beneath it, watching and listening as others use a creation no longer his. Earlier, engineers had organized themselves into such regional associations as New York's American Society of Civil Engineers (1852), which admitted interested amateurs as well as practicing professionals. By 1867 the ASCE had begun to expand geographically and regulate more thoroughly; in 1895 membership was restricted to those who actually designed machinery or public works.

Similar changes had taken place in every profession. For example, medical practitioners, a more or less disreputable group until the mid–nineteenth century, organized themselves into the American Medical Association in 1847 and, by putting into effect strict requirements for education, licensing, and practice, created the demigod image of "the doctor" with its connotations of power, privilege, and esteem. Likewise, the American Bar Association was founded in 1878 and made possible the rise of lawyers to a position in American culture second only to that of physicians. And in 1857 educators formed the National Education Association, a group that, presumably, would have denied a teaching certificate to young Herman Melville, fresh from the decks of the *St. Lawrence.*

Among writers, of course, there was no such formal organizing, although, as James's ruminations show, there was, during the second half-century, a pronounced and often anxious awareness on the part of writers that the production, packaging, and promotion of literature had changed radically. Perhaps there is no more famous comment on the new situation than the one made by Nathaniel Hawthorne in an 1855 letter to his publisher, William D. Ticknor, in which the novelist complained that "America is now wholly given over to a d——d mob of scribbling women." The novel whose success particularly incensed Hawthorne was an 1854 moralistic romance by Maria Susanna Cummins about a Boston orphan girl who is befriended by a virtuous lamplighter. "What is the mystery of these innumerable editions of *The Lamplighter,*" asked Hawthorne, "and other books neither better nor worse?" Of course, one of these "other books" was *The Scarlet Letter* (1850), published by the firm of Ticknor and Fields. *The Lamplighter* had been published by John P. Jewett, which had also published one of the bestselling books of the decade, *Uncle Tom's Cabin* (1852). So in complaining about the "d——d mob," Hawthorne may have been taking a not-so-subtle dig at the relatively poor performance of his own publisher.

For Jewett had, indeed, accomplished a small miracle in his packaging and promoting of *The Lamplighter*, mainly by increasing the number of potential buyers through the targeting of additional readerships. The plot of the novel was already custom-made for consumption by nineteenth-century fiction's target audience, the middle-class woman. This story of self-sacrifice and feminine virtue fulfilled the Horatian requirement that art both entertain and instruct; thus it was not only an acceptable novel but also one that a woman could recommend to her friends as a productive way to fill their leisure hours. What Jewett did was extend the book's appeal to readerships beyond this traditional middle-class female one. Soon after *The Lamplighter* appeared, it became available in a number of different formats: as a child's book with an abridged plot and pictures; as a lavishly illustrated deluxe edition for art lovers; and as an inexpensive "railroad edition" intended for travelers.

These new sales strategies were complemented and made even more successful by a fundamental change in the reviewing industry, one that reflects the increasing rigidification of American industry generally. The midcentury growth of the audience for fiction was paralleled by an increase in newspaper and periodical publication; moreover, the two phenomena were joined by a strong moral bond, to judge by the comments of most reviewers. The prevailing view was that fiction was a didactic medium with a clear mandate to instruct readers. After all, the novel as it is known now was then but a few decades old and therefore somewhat suspect, especially in contrast to the more venerable essay and poem. So novelists, publishers, reviewers, and readers interested in increasing the odds of survival for this vulnerable form resorted to various strategies designed to give it a fighting chance in the market. One such strategy was to pretend that the work of fiction was factual or at least fact-based. Poe's *Narrative of Arthur Gordon Pym* was passed off as an autobiography, for example, and Hawthorne's *Scarlet Letter* is preceded by a lengthy preface detailing the author's "discovery" of the actual letter in an old trunk. And in cases where pretense at veracity was pointless, the case was often made that the book in question was fiction, yes, but of a highly moral kind not only unlikely to lead the reader astray (especially the young or female reader) but also capable of delivering an uplifting moral message.

Logically, then, reviewers were seen as obliged to provide direction for readers, a significant portion of whom were not thought capable of making informed decisions on their own. Worse, fiction readers were assumed to be less intellectually endowed than readers of nonfiction and more indolent and desultory in their reading habits. A writer in the November 1859 number of *DeBow's Review* described the fiction-reading public as one that "cannot understand or appreciate . . . refined or elevated sentiment, original and profound thought" and for whom "the commonplace, the superficial, the sensual, the gross, and the gaudy, are alone adapted to their torpid intellectual tastes." Even as late as April 1865, these sentiments are echoed in the *Ladies' Repository*, where it is reported that "hurrying, uncultured, every-day people . . . will not read heavy, labored, theological works"; the masses "must have easy reading, or they will not read at all."

Inevitably, this untenable situation changed as both lay readers and reviewers became more discriminating in their choices and less enchanted with the shoddy offerings of the publishing industry. Susan S. Williams quotes an excerpt from the *American Publishers' Circular and Literary Gazette* (1855) that describes this reformation: "A few years since . . . the nation seemed, for a time, in danger

of becoming a land of novelists. . . . Bookmaking became conta-
gious. One successful production . . . called into existence from ten
to forty trashy and stupid imitations of it. They were all puffed,
and, probably, all sold. But the public at length awoke; it discov-
ered the deception. Then came the reaction. A great many books
were published, but no system of puffery or advertising could in-
duce men to buy them." Slower to react, the reviewing industry
nonetheless came around as well to this proliferation of shoddy
work: "The critics, too, gradually assumed a tone of caution. They
found their opinions disrespected; they resolved to change their
tactics; and although we are now, as it were, but in one period of
transition, it is not difficult, we think, to behold the dawn of a more
healthful and secure existence" (192).

During this "period of transition," reviewers took pains not only
to discriminate more carefully between good fiction and bad but
also to describe more precisely the books that came across their
desks. The critical reception of *The Lamplighter* reveals both an
awareness of the contemporary moralizing condescension toward
readers as well as the reviewers' desire to improve their own standards and acquire the rigor (and the public respect that accompa-
nied it) that had become the hallmark of other professions. At the
time, as Nina Baym observes, it was commonplace to categorize
popular novels as belonging to one of three classes: the metropoli-
tan novel, or novel of low life; the domestic novel; and the fashionable novel, or novel of high life. Nominally, *The Lamplighter*
belonged to the middle group, though reviewers, aware of the
disreputation into which their trade had fallen, were careful to
distinguish it from similar novels that were merely melodramatic
or sensational. In the March 28, 1854, number of the *New York
Tribune*, for example, it is noted that Cummins had dealt "with
the materials at hand less with the view of enforcing a moral,
than as the legitimate subjects of literary art." Thus the aggressive
and ingenious publishing strategies of John P. Jewett and others,

combined with reviewers' awareness of the growing sophistication of the audience for fiction as well as their own need for higher standards, helped to make *The Lamplighter* extraordinarily successful. Add to this the popular stage productions of the work in Boston and, later, London, and it is easy to see the importance of one work that not only typified the mass-appeal novel that dominated the midcentury but also anticipated the novel of "literary art" that achieved greater prominence as the century went on.

As readers and reviewers became more sophisticated, both groups began to think of fiction as art and not merely moral instruction. With this change came an increase in interest in such writerly conventions as character and the rise of the novel that was character-driven rather than plot-driven. James L. Machor reports that, in the early days of American book reviewing, it was assumed that novels were narrated by the novelists themselves, and therefore the novelist should be a moral authority whom the reader could trust. Certainly this could be said of the Maria Cummins, who was taken by readers to be a good woman telling a story in which goodness prevails, even if the characters in that story are rudimentary and forgettable. But for a later novelist like Mark Twain, for example, authorial morality is much less important than character complexity. Hence the appeal, in Twain's day, of the Tom Sawyer who not only dominated the story of his own adventures (1876) but also played a crucial role in *The Adventures of Huckleberry Finn* (1884) and then returned in *Tom Sawyer Abroad* (1894) and *Tom Sawyer, Detective* (1896). Richard Hill points out that Tom may not be popular in contemporary academe, but he was an unadulterated hero to both the fictional citizens of St. Petersburg and the readers of Twain's day: the bravest, smartest kid in town, the one who not only saves the judge's daughter from a horrible death but wins the pot of robber's gold, a literary authority, and, as the premier practitioner of the imaginative hoax, a performance artist *non pareil*. In Hill's words, Tom is "full of the heroic pioneer spirit, the give-me-liberty-or-give-me-death, I-only-regret-I-have-one-life-to-give-for-my-country, damn-the-torpedoes-full-speed-ahead American Right Stuff."

Contemporary reviewers of *Huckleberry Finn*, whose hero was billed as "Tom Sawyer's Comrade" on the cover, were so taken with Tom that they were blind to the racism of the novel's last chapters. In examining dozens of reviews written between 1885 and 1900, Hill found only one that condemned the ending; more typical was the review that read, "The romantic side of Tom Sawyer is shown in most delightfully humorous fashion in the account of his difficult devices to aid in the easy escape of Jim, a runaway negro." African American novelists, too, had to take into account prevailing racial attitudes in the presentation of their characters. In Frederick Douglass's short novel *The Heroic Slave* (1853), the black hero is introduced by an authoritative white character who, in effect, vouches for him, simultaneously empowering and limiting his voice. As late as 1899, this same frame technique is used in Charles Waddell Chesnutt's *The Conjure Woman*, in which a white northerner buys a plantation and inherits an ex-slave named Uncle Julius, whose buffoonish tales comprise the novel. Characters like Uncle Julius strike readers as embarrassing now, though, in Chesnutt's day, they represent a calculated authorial response to a contemporary readership's resistance to anything remotely resembling black aggression.

Thus the novel, which, at the beginning of the century, was viewed more or less amateurishly by writer, reader, and reviewer alike, had undergone a serious transformation in the middle and, by the end, become "literature." With success, however, comes first self-consciousness and then anxiety: fear that one has failed to live up to one's own standards, nervousness about the reception of one's work. Henry James was not only one of the greatest novelists of any country or time; he was also one of the great worriers as well as one of the prodigious recorders of his own concerns. In contrast to Hawthorne's occasional muttering on the subject, James fretted constantly about audience, sales, and every conceivable aspect of the publishing process, as his journals and letters reveal. And in one of his novels, he dramatizes his fear that perhaps the novel had become too successful, that the new strategies for sales, distribution, and review had created a kind of novel so highly evolved that it had become estranged from its original audience.

With such novels as *The Portrait of a Lady* (1881), James had already shown that he was a committed realist in the tradition of Flaubert. But in midcareer, he detoured into naturalism, an unusual mode for a novelist whose work dealt almost exclusively with the aristocratic and the wealthy. *The Princess Casamassima* (1886) is the story of Hyacinth Robinson, a cultured if impoverished bookbinder who joins a band of revolutionaries but kills himself when ordered to assassinate a duke. Margaret Scanlan points out that Hyacinth, the illegitimate son of a poor Frenchwoman and English nobleman, contains within himself the struggle between political action and high culture, and, although he leans more toward the latter than the former, it is not mere fastidiousness that keeps him from his bloody deed. Instead, Hyacinth's suicide is an admission of the failure of revolutionaries who cannot win an audience they claim to represent—like a novelist whom no one reads.

Writers, readers, and publishers had succeeded in not only making fiction respectable and profitable but had conferred upon it the status of high art. As the peak of his career, James was competing with bestselling popular writers as well as so-called art novelists like himself. The industry had never been healthier, but then the field had never been more crowded, the demands for excellence never higher. No wonder one novelist, at least, was wondering whether all this success was worth it.

It Isn't about America, It *Is* America

MARK TWAIN'S *HUCKLEBERRY FINN*

According to Twain's definition of a classic as a book that everybody praises and nobody talks about, *The Adventures of Huckleberry Finn* (1885) hardly qualifies for classic status, since it is a book everybody talks about and almost nobody praises, unless they do so with serious reservations. In an essay that articulates a widespread contemporary attitude toward Twain's masterpiece, Greil Marcus argues that while *Huckleberry Finn* "may be the carrier of our national soul, it is also the carrier of our national poison: the word 'nigger.' " This last part is unarguable; passages that portray the runaway slave Jim as childlike and depict his constant humiliation, especially at the hands of the two boys he calls friends, are impossible to read without cringing. The question of the masterpiece's flaw is settled, then. What remains to consider is the extent to which it is a masterpiece—in other words, how well does Twain's novel function as "the carrier of our national soul"?

There is no denying that *Huckleberry Finn* is Twain's greatest success as a writer. To that point in his career, Twain had written an undisputed classic of children's literature, *The Adventures of Tom Sawyer* (1876), a nostalgic tale of boyish adventure in a town much like the Hannibal, Missouri, Twain had grown up in. But most of his books were thinly veiled accounts of his travels: *The Innocents Abroad* (1869), which deals with the Mediterranean and the Holy Land; *Roughing It* (1872), an account of his time in the West; *A*

Tramp Abroad (1880), which focuses on a walking tour through Germany and Switzerland; and *Life on the Mississippi* (1880), a re-creation of Twain's days as a riverboat pilot. If the so-called "matter of Hannibal" fueled Twain's best writing, the travel narrative attracted him in a way that the more static material did not. Twain's genius was to combine in *Huckleberry Finn* the stuff of childhood memories with the story of a boy and a man on a sometimes frightening, sometimes idyllic voyage down the Mississippi River. Moreover, he added a third and completely new element that propelled his new book beyond the limitations of children's literature and humor, a moral dimension that peaks in Huck's decision to let Jim go free and his famous statement, uttered as he realizes that he is defying the white, Christian, slaveholding morality of his day, "All right, then, I'll *go* to hell."

Huckleberry Finn was a radical novel when published, one in which Twain attacked everything America held dear—family, religion, politics, money—through the person of an illiterate twelve-year-old. Immediately, the novel was attacked because of the character of Huck, who was seen as a poor example for America's children. A typical notice appeared in the March 2 issue of the *New York World*, where it is noted that only Twain's established reputation as a humorist saves "this cheap and pernicious stuff" from complete condemnation. The story is one of "a wretchedly low, vulgar, sneaking and lying Southern country boy" who, in the company of "a runaway negro" and a pair of "impostors" (the King and the Duke), practices an "irreverence which makes parents, guardians and people who are at all good and proper ridiculous." Victor Fischer observes that negative reviews of *Huckleberry Finn* were consistent in criticizing Twain for making light of lying in a book seemingly written for children and that this was the reason given for banning the novel from a number of libraries well into the early twentieth century.

In the last half of the twentieth century and into the twenty-first, of course, *Huckleberry Finn* has regularly been the subject of calls for removal from classrooms and libraries, not because of its endorsement of Huck's mischief but for its racist portrayal of Jim. Ironically, as Shelley Fisher Fishkin and others have pointed out, Twain drew on African American source materials in composing the novel, although, to the reviewers of Twain's day, who were preoccupied with Huck, Jim seems like a forerunner of Ralph Ellison's Invisible Man. Now, of course, it is impossible to overlook the condescension of the final chapters, in which Tom Sawyer reappears to re-enslave Jim while the morally reborn Huck reverts to his old status as Tom's passive sidekick and Twain's epic turns into a farce. The objectionable final chapters of the novel have led scholars like Guy Cardwell to say that Twain must now be viewed as a representative American figure rather than a heroic one, a writer who, if he "helped to make America's culture . . . was also its prisoner."

In answer to Hemingway's citation of *Huckleberry Finn* as the source for all subsequent American literature, novelist Jane Smiley has said it would have been better had that source been Harriet Beecher Stowe's *Uncle Tom's Cabin* (1852), with its "thoughtful, autonomous, and passionate black characters," which prompted Roy Blount Jr.'s response that this is like saying it would be better for people to come from heaven than from sex. There have been various retellings of the story of Huck and Jim, including John Seelye's *The True Adventures of Huckleberry Finn* (1970) and Greg Matthews's *The Further Adventures of Huckleberry Finn* (1983), although, as African American author David Bradley points out, no one has been able to write a better ending to Twain's novel or, for that matter, to the story of blacks and whites together in America. For better or worse, *The Adventures of Huckleberry Finn* is truly the carrier of our national soul. The book isn't about America—it *is* America.

What Is a Book?

In the middle of the journey of our life, I found myself in a dark wood, asking myself a question, namely, "What is the canon?" On my way to answering it, I'd like to say I went to hell and purgatory and paradise, like Dante, but all I did was give up on my first question and substitute another, better one that serves as the title to this essay. And I think I have an answer to that one.

Some background. In 1987, Allan Bloom published *The Closing of the American Mind*, in which he argued against multiculturalism in the classroom and for the traditional Western canon as most people define it, that is, a list of works beginning with Plato and Aristotle and continuing through Hume, Kant, and Nietzsche. No doubt to even Bloom's surprise, *The Closing of the American Mind* spent thirty-one weeks at the top of the bestseller list, ultimately selling more than 800,000 copies and spawning a micro-industry of responses both positive and negative.

Among recent books that take up Bloom's argument, the best known are probably David Denby's *Great Books: My Adventures with Homer, Rousseau, Woolf, and Other Indestructible Writers of the Western World* and Lawrence W. Levine's *The Opening of the American Mind: Canons, Culture, and History*, both published in 1996. These two titles make clear where the authors' sympathies lie: at loggerheads. They also suggest that, like the poor, the canon will always be with us, both as a monument to cultural achievement and also a whipping post to which past oppressors can be tied and then flogged by present-day champions of their oppressees.

Okay, so what is the canon? Or is there a canon? Or are there different canons for different audiences? And who decides? A recent attempt at canon-making is described in a November 27, 1996, *New York Times* article describing a survey taken by Professor Kenneth Dauber of the State University of New York at Buffalo, who asked his more than 2,100 colleagues what ten literary works they would most like their own children to have read by the time they finished college. According to Professor Dauber, putting the question this way (as opposed to simply asking for the ten most important books ever written, say) resulted in a response "more primal than political." On the other hand, the results were political anyway because the top ten books were all written by dead white men—hardly a surprise, notes the professor, since "our faculty is comprised principally of *live* white men."

As reported in the *Times,* the SUNY-Buffalo faculty's top ten books include, in no apparent order, Freud's *Interpretation of Dreams;* Darwin's *Origin of Species;* the Bible; Shakespeare's *Hamlet;* Dickens's *Great Expectations;* Plato's *Republic;* Homer's *Iliad* or *Odyssey;* Melville's *Moby-Dick;* a collection of the Declaration of Independence, the Constitution, and the Federalist Papers; and, finally, an unnamed Tolstoy novel. This is a worthy list, of course, if a strangely skewed one.

For example, there are no recent books; the newest is Freud's, which appeared in 1900. Too, with the exception of *Hamlet,* none of these works was written between the second century and 1776. Where are the works by, on the one hand, Augustine, Aquinas, Dante, Boccaccio, and Montaigne, and, on the other, Joyce, Eliot, Woolf, and Hemingway? One quick conclusion that can be drawn from a list like Professor Dauber's is that, if you list ten great books, you've got to leave out ten or a hundred or a thousand that are equally great.

I didn't let that stop me from deciding to reproduce Professor Dauber's effort on my own campus, though on a very small scale—

using twenty faculty, say. I wanted to keep things simple for several reasons, not the least of which was my own lack of expertise as a pollster; twenty responses would be no problem, I figured, but not a hundred times that many.

By limiting the size of my sample, I also wondered if I couldn't correct for the bias that Professor Dauber admits to in his results by selecting a deliberately more diverse group than his. Too, it struck me that there is possibly an additional and unacknowledged problem with the professor's group, which is that, SUNY-Buffalo's admirable reputation notwithstanding, there must be quite a range of literary aptitudes among his numerous colleagues, from the highly developed to the less so. That, I knew, would not be a problem with my smaller group, since I could select not only for diversity but also quality as well.

Of the nineteen faculty members I eventually chose for my survey, most of whom were from either the English Department or the Department of Modern Languages, seventeen have what the academy considers the terminal degree, that is, either the Ph.D. or M.F.A. Of the remaining two, one is working on a Ph.D. and the other has a master's degree. On the whole, they're a highly accomplished group: sixteen have published one or more books. Most importantly, though, these were among the best-read people of my acquaintance; each of them is a prodigious buyer of books of every kind, and they all have what Thomas Jefferson called "a canine appetite" for reading. In fact, the lone master's-degree holder in my group is there for just that reason: of all my colleagues, she reads the most and the most widely.

As far as cultural diversity goes, ten of the nineteen are women, three are African American, one Cuban American, and one is a native of the Netherlands. The most important aspect of their diversity, though, is that this group covers a variety of historical periods, from medieval to contemporary, and a variety of literatures, from American and English to French, Italian, and Spanish.

Having made up my list of faculty respondents, I realized I had two captive audiences on whom I could perform the same experiment: the students in my classes. There were twenty-eight juniors and seniors in my nineteenth-century U.S. novel course, and I was also teaching a graduate writing seminar with twenty-one students in it, most of whom were poets or fiction writers themselves. In other words, as student groups go, these two were fairly sophisticated, though surely their responses would be different from those of the faculty, and that difference, I thought, might be instructive in some as-yet-unforeseen way. Then, having expanded my initial survey group from one to three, I figured I'd go one step further and poll a fourth group as well, a high-school advanced placement English class of twenty-eight students.

From the outset, I was aware of how little science was involved in my data gathering. There was a certain amount of planning, of course, but most of my time was spent cajoling and arm-twisting and trying to get people to give me their lists; anyone who has ever sent a memo to a faculty and tried to get them to reply by a deadline will know what I am talking about. So there was a lot of jawboning, yes, but scarcely more science than it takes to make a lemon-meringue pie and certainly less than is required to program a VCR.

Indeed, if an objective response to the survey question involves a certain amount of thoughtful reflection, I insisted on just the opposite, that is, a nearly instant response that would, I hoped, fulfill Professor Dauber's expectation of a primal reaction rather than one governed by considerations of which books would look good on such a list, which would be most enlightening, and so on.

The three classes, of course, were at my mercy: I told the students to make a rough list at the beginning of the period and then I collected their formal lists at the end. To the faculty I said that I wanted their lists by the end of the day, a stipulation some met and many did not. I finally tracked one slowpoke down in his office and sat by his desk while he wrote down his titles. When he finished, he thanked me for giving him only ten minutes because, as he said, if he'd had fifteen, he wouldn't have been able to do it.

The question I posed to each of my four groups was the same as the one used in the SUNY-Buffalo survey: "What ten books would you like your own children to have read by the time they finish college?" Here are the results, beginning with the youngest age group and proceeding to the oldest (the order is determined by the number of times each book was mentioned, with books receiving equal numbers of mentions listed together in alphabetical order; for example, in the first list, the Chopin and Heller novels are equally popular and so are listed as 3 and 4):

Twenty-five High-School Students, Advanced Placement
English Class

1	Salinger, *The Catcher in the Rye*
2	Hurston, *Their Eyes Were Watching God*
3, 4	Chopin, *The Awakening*
	Heller, *Catch-22*
5, 6, 7	Remarque, *All Quiet on the Western Front*
	Shakespeare, *Romeo and Juliet*
	Wright, *Black Boy*
8, 9	Dickens, *A Tale of Two Cities*
	Fitzgerald, *The Great Gatsby*
10	Alcott, *Little Women*
	Bradbury, *Fahrenheit 451*
	Camus, *The Stranger*
	Dickens, *Great Expectations*
	Lee, *To Kill a Mockingbird*
	Shakespeare, *Othello*
	White, *Charlotte's Web*
	Williams, *A Streetcar Named Desire*

I couldn't help noticing that at least nine of the works on this list have been made into movies, including *William Shakespeare's Romeo and Juliet*, which stars teen heartthrobs Leonardo DiCaprio and Claire Danes and was in the theaters at the time I conducted my survey. I suspected the students had been shown others in their classes and wondered if the impact of visual images had made these "texts" more memorable than others.

In talking with the high-school students later, I had a conversation with one young woman that I found amusing, though what she said kept recurring to me throughout my data-gathering and, in the end, proved the key to the question posed by the title of this essay. She asked me if I knew of a book called *The Phantom Tollbooth*, and I said, yes, I'd seen it in the bookstore, and is it a good one? It's the best, she said, absolutely the best; she'd read it in the fifth grade and then maybe two dozen times in the next two years and had put it on her list.

But since she hadn't read *The Phantom Tollbooth* in five years, I suggested gently she might read it again and see if it's as good as she remembers, because people mature, tastes change, and . . . at this point she cut me off and said, I don't *have* to read it again, and she tapped her head furiously to show me where the book lived: not on some dusty book shelf, but in the unsullied world of her imagination.

When I looked at the high-schoolers' surveys later, I saw that some of them seemed to reveal a great deal about particular respondents. One youngster listed *The Catcher in the Rye*, *A Tale of Two Cities*, *The Awakening*, and *The Scarlet Letter* but also *How to Win Friends and Influence People*, *Seven Habits of Highly Effective People*, *The Magic of Thinking Big*, *Think and Grow Rich*, *Chicken Soup for the Soul*, and *How to Have Confidence and Power in Dealing with People*. A surprising number of these students listed books by Dr. Seuss and other children's authors, and three of them listed *Anthem,* which I'd never heard of and learned later was by Ayn Rand.

Now for the second list:

Twenty-eight College Seniors, Nineteenth-Century U.S. Novel Class

1, 2, 3   Hawthorne, *The Scarlet Letter*
           Jacobs, *Incidents in the Life of a Slave Girl*
           Shakespeare, *Plays* (especially *Hamlet* and *A Midsummer Night's Dream*)

4, 5, 6   Poe, *Narrative of Arthur Gordon Pym of Nantucket*
           Salinger, *The Catcher in the Rye*
           Vonnegut, *Slaughterhouse Five*

7, 8, 9   Chopin, *The Awakening and Other Stories*
           James, *The Turn of the Screw*
           Twain, *The Adventures of Huckleberry Finn*

10   The Bible
           Hurston, *Their Eyes Were Watching God*
           Lee, *To Kill a Mockingbird*
           Morrison, *Beloved*

Five of these titles are ones I was teaching to these students at this time, which should remind the reader of my comment about science and lemon pie, above. On the other hand, they are all good books, and I would have no reason not to recommend them. Probably the least-known of these is Harriet Jacobs's *Incidents in the Life of a Slave Girl,* which has always been a real eye-opener for my students since its author was herself a slave and therefore speaks authentically about the horrors of a life that contemporaries like Harriet Beecher Stowe could only describe from the outside. Is this what a good book is, one that makes a difference in how we see the world?

As with the high-school survey, the college one too contained its little surprises and major bafflements. For some reason, Dr. Seuss's books kept showing up, but then so did Laclos's *Liaisons danger-*

euses, Lewis's *The Monk,* and Mann's *Dr. Faustus.* One student listed Boethius's *Consolation of Philosophy* but also Vonnegut's *Slaughterhouse Five,* that being possibly the first instance of those two books ever appearing on the same page together.

Here's the third list:

Twenty-one College Students, Graduate Writing Seminar

1	Shakespeare, *Hamlet*
2, 3	The Bible
	Melville, *Moby-Dick*
4	Twain, *The Adventures of Huckleberry Finn*
5, 6, 7	Conrad, *Heart of Darkness*
	Faulkner, *The Sound and the Fury*
	Dostoevsky, *Crime and Punishment*
8, 9, 10	Eliot, *The Waste Land and Other Poems*
	Faulkner, *The Hamlet*
	Hemingway, *Collected Stories*
	Salinger, *The Catcher in the Rye*
	Shakespeare, *King Lear*
	Steinbeck, *The Grapes of Wrath*

As I moved from readers in their teens and early twenties to ones in their late twenties and over, the lists became not only more canonical but also more homogeneous—no more Boethius or Vonnegut, together or even singly. I wondered if, since the grad students were writers (mainly of fiction) as well as readers, they had listed certain craft models who may have been important to them: Hemingway for style, say, and Faulkner for interior monologue.

Finally, the fourth list:

Nineteen Faculty from English and Modern Language Departments

1	Shakespeare, *Plays* (especially *King Lear*)
2	Ellison, *Invisible Man*
3, 4	Eliot, *Middlemarch*

	Melville, *Moby-Dick*
5	The Bible
6, 7, 8	Eliot, *The Waste Land and Other Poems*
	Homer, *The Odyssey*
	Twain, *The Adventures of Huckleberry Finn*
9, 10	Dante, *The Inferno*
	García Márquez, *One Hundred Years of Solitude*
	Morrison, *Beloved*
	Wright, *Native Son*

For the first time, I saw the names of Dante, Homer, and García Márquez—younger readers, evidently there is more to heaven and earth than is dreamt of in your book lists. As I expected, the faculty came through with the most canonical list of all, even though, as I look at their recommendations, I can't help but be bothered again by the problem of defining "canon" in the first place. Boethius and Vonnegut don't try to bunk together here, but do Shakespeare and Richard Wright make compatible bedfellows? T. S. Eliot appears on this list, which raises another question: where has lyric poetry been hiding so far?

Not at all satisfied with my four very different lists, I decided to make a master list. There are two ways to do this, I realized. Here is the first:

The Four Lists Combined

	Salinger, *The Catcher in the Rye*
1, 2	Shakespeare, *Plays* (especially *Hamlet, A Midsummer Night's Dream,* and *King Lear*)
3	The Bible
4, 5, 6	Chopin, *The Awakening and Other Stories*
	Melville, *Moby-Dick*
	Twain, *The Adventures of Huckleberry Finn*
7	Hurston, *Their Eyes Were Watching God*
8, 9	Hawthorne, *The Scarlet Letter*

Jacobs, *Incidents in the Life of a Slave Girl*
10   Poe, *Narrative of Arthur Gordon Pym of Nantucket*
Vonnegut, *Slaughterhouse Five*

It might be argued that this method of combining makes a stripling's vote equal to a graybeard's, but, since I was trying to make this exercise credible to students, this radically democratic vote-counting method was an important selling point. A hodgepodge of titles with a definite tilt to the modern, this first master list should offer some satisfaction to both the egalitarian (most great-books lists consist entirely of white males, but at least this one has three women authors, two of whom are African Americans) as well as the canonical (this list includes both the Bible and Shakespeare). In other words, this list will satisfy no one.

The second master list can be made this way:

All Ninety-three Individual Ballots Combined
1   Shakespeare, *Plays* (especially *Hamlet, A Midsummer
            Night's Dream,* and *King Lear*)
2   Salinger, *The Catcher in the Rye*
3   Hurston, *Their Eyes Were Watching God*
4   The Bible
5   Twain, *The Adventures of Huckleberry Finn*
6   Chopin, *The Awakening and Other Stories*
7   Melville, *Moby-Dick*
8, 9   Ellison, *Invisible Man*
Hawthorne, *The Scarlet Letter*
10   Fitzgerald, *The Great Gatsby*
Jacobs, *Incidents in the Life of a Slave Girl*

Again, this is a list unlikely to please anyone, though there are some interesting differences between it and the others. For one thing, the rankings of individual books are much more distinct. For example, Shakespeare got forty-five votes to Salinger's twenty-five, and only two books (*Invisible Man* and *The Scarlet Letter*) got the same number of votes. As far as names go, this master list differs from the other because Poe and Vonnegut are dropped and Ellison and Fitzgerald added.

As I looked over my four initial lists, I had these initial reactions:

1. In deciding what books are important, how big a part does nostalgia play? Notice that *The Catcher in the Rye* is high on the high-school list, lower on the undergraduate list, lowest on the graduate one, and then it disappears. Think of the conversation I had with the high-schooler about *The Phantom Toolbooth* and then consider this: have the students who listed *Catcher* read it recently or are they remembering it as a one of their first big satisfying reads?

2. Only one high-schooler listed the Bible, even though my guess is that a rather high percentage of these students read the Bible weekly when they go to church or temple. Guessing again, I would venture that members of the three older groups are likely to be more indifferent to religion than the high-school students are, even though significant numbers of each of the older groups did include the Bible on their lists. In other words, whereas many older readers think of the Bible as a book written like any other, subject to interpretation like other books, and so on, almost none of the youngest group does, and this despite its colloquial definition as "the Good Book," a phrase they're surely familiar with. It could also be that, with more reading experience under their belts, the older groups recognize how important the Bible is as a key to other, subsequent books.

3. As I compiled the results, the popular titles soon became less interesting than the exceptions to me, and I soon wearied of see-ing the same titles move to the center. After all, I've read most of these not only often but also recently, whereas it's been a long time since I've read all of *The Oresteia* and *Don Quixote*, and I've never read *A Vindication of the Rights of Woman, The Incredible*

Lightness of Being, or *The Pillow Book of Sei Shonagon.* By the way, when I handed out my surveys, I didn't ask for annotations, but I certainly got them, and no one was more zealous than the person who mentioned the last-named book. For what it's worth, then, let me pass along the information that you shouldn't really think of yourself as an educated person unless you've read *The Pillow Book of Sei Shonagon.*

4. As they say on the street, Shakespeare's da man. If you take the author-is-dead pronouncements of Roland Barthes and Michel Foucault literally, the Bard's a goner. But he's alive in the hearts and minds of my ninety-three book-lovers, and in the surveys, his works came in way ahead of anybody else's.

The MIAs include Hardy, Trollope, Thackeray, and Austen (and with all those recent film adaptations of her novels, too). Dickens is on the high-school list (twice, in fact), but none of the other Victorians. And where are the authors of the seventeenth and eighteenth centuries, of the 250-year period between *King Lear* and *Moby-Dick*?

The biggest omission, though, is poetry. When I passed out my survey forms to the graduate students, one graduate student said, Oh, we can't list poems. Like what? I said. And she said, "Ode on a Grecian Urn," so I said, Just put down Keats's *Collected Odes.* But her lament did identify a problem: because we teach poems one at a time, most readers think of specific poem titles rather than collections. Only one person of the ninety-three listed *The Norton Anthology of Poetry*—is this because we think of favorite books as pals, as good friends to curl up with, and nobody ever curled up with an anthology?

The more I thought about it, the more this anthropomorphizing of books seemed crucial to me in dictating my respondents' choices. For example, when I remembered what the high-school student said to me about *The Phantom Tollbooth* and the way she had defended it against my suggestion that it might somehow be unworthy of inclusion on a list of important books, I realized, from the language she chose and the facial expressions and hand gestures she used, that she was standing up for that book the way she might have stood up for a goofy but lovable brother or smart, dorky friend.

One of the graduate students suggested that the overall supremacy of Shakespeare on everyone's list is proof that the French poststructuralists and their followers are wrong, that the Dead White European Male is more alive now than ever before. My own feeling is that the concept of authorship is almost irrelevant to a survey like this. What counts is the personhood, not of the author, but of the book: whether there was or wasn't a historical person named Shakespeare and whether he did or didn't write *Romeo and Juliet* is less important than the fact that the play itself is a person, a wise and generous pal who is somehow both young and old at once and who tells you more about love and family and the feelings people have and the mistakes they make than you'd ever get from a stadium full of parents and coaches and counselors and psychologists.

The more I looked at my lists and thought about the things that my respondents said to me, the more I realized that they had turned real books into figurative persons, much as books become people in one of the high-schoolers' favorites, Ray Bradbury's *Fahrenheit 451*. Surely this is why the novel is the genre that occurs most often on these lists. The novel is a friend like any other: steadfast, there when you need him or her, friendly to you but in need of your friendship (that is, your sympathetic reading) as well. The earliest novels were people, in effect: *Pamela* is Richardson's heroine writing for help, and *Robinson Crusoe* is an outcast telling you of his trials (which you've had, too) and triumphs (and you've a few of those as well).

The other literary genres are less flesh-and-blood than the novel is. A play is a temporary confection, as Puck reminds us at the end of *A Midsummer Night's Dream*, an array of "visions," a "dream" created by players who are themselves "shadows." (The most popular plays on the lists are biographies, though, of Romeo and Juliet, Hamlet, and Lear—people, in other words). A poem is a quick chat over the fence with a neighbor, someone who is smarter than you are and maybe even a little intimidating, whereas a novel is familiar and domestic, a week- or month-long presence on your end table or by your bed.

Just as we all have different tastes in friends, nonfiction will always be cozier to some readers than others, and my lists did include Plato's *Symposium,* Aristotle's *Poetics,* Montaigne's *Essays,* and Descartes's *Meditations on First Philosophy.* But we like persons best, especially first persons, which may explain why Ishmael, Huck Finn, Nick Carraway, and Holden Caulfield are on this list as well as the first-person narrators of Ellison's *Invisible Man,* Poe's *Pym,* and Jacobs's *Incidents.* The younger my respondents were, the more novels they listed: often my own students seem to want me to be a father to them, and I think they want their books to be like a benign parent, too. Or perhaps more like an uncle or aunt, say: wise, tolerant, supportive but not demanding.

This essay began with an attempt at defining the canon and ends as an attempt at defining a book. As a result of doing my survey, the whole idea of the canon seems less important to me now. Apparently Professor Dauber of SUNY-Buffalo is satisfied with the list of books that he drew up with the help of his colleagues; the *New York Times* article reported that he was going to teach a course in the spring 1997 term called "The Top Ten Books," based on the results of his survey. More power to him! It's a terrific list as well as one which, if you're a scientist, was obviously constituted in a much more reliable manner than any list of mine.

Still, I have a certain affection for my looser, more populist attempt at canon formation, precisely because the end result is no canon at all. It's the diversity of the books my individual respondents recommended that appeals to me; while I learned something about readers' tastes (and Shakespeare's popularity), right now I'd still rather read *The Pillow Book of Sei Shonagon* than reread *Macbeth*. Also, I'd like to conduct this survey again in five years, ten, twenty, and see what, if any, differences there are between the lists I come up with and the ones I have now. The canon is a destination; I'm more interested in the trip.

I hope others will read this essay and do something similar and let me know what they find. I hope other, nonacademic readers do a comparable survey with their book-club members or local library patrons. I'd like to see somebody redress the poetry imbalance and find out what the top ten lyric poems are. Or what about "the ten books that changed your life"? I bring up this possibility because one faculty respondent told me she put *Middlemarch* on her list because she'd first read it just as she was about to enter into a bad marriage, and when she saw how important it is to choose a husband carefully, she called the whole thing off.

Or how about, not the ten books you'd want your children to read, but the ten you'd want to discuss with your children? How about a wild-card list: pass out copies of one of the master lists and tell everybody they have to put down only books they don't see there?

So I learned a lot by conducting my survey the way I did, by asking those who were sixteen as well as sixty, who'd read maybe forty books in their lives or as many as four thousand. The little people are as good as the big shots in this country, the masses as good as their leaders: that's the American way. That's one of the reasons why, on my own top-ten list, I put Whitman's *Leaves of Grass*.

No one else did, though.

Bibliography

For the sake of convenience, works are cited briefly by title (and, where chronology is crucial, date of publication) within the essays themselves. The following citations give more complete bibliographical information on the cited texts and, in some cases, suggestions for further reading.

What Is a Writer?

BREAKFAST WITH THE CUMAEAN SIBYL, OR A POET'S EDUCATION

Attridge, Derek. *Poetic Rhythm: An Introduction.* New York: Cambridge University Press, 1995.

Corn, Alfred. *The Poem's Heartbeat: A Manual of Prosody.* Brownsville, Oreg.: Story Line Press, 1997.

Hartman, Charles O. *Virtual Muse: Experiments in Computer Poetry.* Hanover, N.H.: University Press of New England, 1996.

Wesling, Donald. *The Scissors of Meter: Grammetrics and Reading.* Ann Arbor: University of Michigan Press, 1996.

DON'T KNOW MUCH ABOUT HISTORY

Howard, Richard. *Like Most Revelations.* New York: Pantheon Books, 1994.

————. *Trappings.* New York: Turtle Point Press, 1999.

Kaufman, Alan, ed. *The Outlaw Bible of American Poetry.* New York: Thunder's Mouth Press, 1999.

Wolf, Robert, ed. *An American Mosaic: Prose and Poetry by Everyday Folk.* New York: Oxford University Press, 1999.

Wright, Charles. *Appalachia*. New York: Farrar, Straus and Giroux, 1998.
———. *Black Zodiac*. New York: Farrar, Straus and Giroux, 1997.
———. *Negative Blue: Selected Later Poems*. New York: Farrar, Straus and Giroux, 2000.

IS THERE A SOUTHERN POETRY?

Ammons, A. R. *Garbage*. New York: Norton, 1993.
Berry, Wendell. *Entries*. New York: Pantheon, 1994.
Braggs, Earl S. *Hat Dancer Blue*. Tallahassee, Fla.: Anhinga, 1992.
Katrovas, Richard. *The Book of Complaints*. Pittsburgh: Carnegie Mellon University Press, 1993.
Ludvigson, Susan. *Everything Winged Must Be Dreaming*. Baton Rouge: Louisiana State University Press, 1993.
Montez, Susan. *Radio Free Queens*. New York: George Braziller, 1994.
Morgan, Elizabeth Seydel. *The Governor of Desire*. Baton Rouge: Louisiana State University Press, 1993.
Rollings, Alane. *The Struggle to Adore*. Brownsville, Oreg.: Story Line Press, 1994.
Smith, Charlie. *The Palms*. New York: Norton, 1993.
Soniat, Katherine. *A Shared Life*. Iowa City: University of Iowa Press, 1993.
Wood, John. *In Primary Light*. Iowa City: University of Iowa Press, 1994.

What Is a Critic?

EMERSON, POE, AND AMERICAN CRITICISM IN THE
NINETEENTH CENTURY

Charvat, William. *The Origins of American Critical Thought, 1810–1835*. Philadelphia: University of Pennsylvania Press, 1936.
Goldsmith, Arnold L. *American Literary Criticism, 1905–1965*. Boston: G. K. Hall, 1979.
Perosa, Sergio. *American Theories of the Novel, 1793–1903*. New York: New York University Press, 1983.
Rathbun, John W. *American Literary Criticism, 1800–1860*. Boston: G. K. Hall, 1979.

Rathbun, John W., and H. H. Clark. *American Literary Criticism, 1860–1905.* Boston: G. K. Hall, 1979.

SLOUCHING TOWARD BALTIMORE

Adams, Hazard, and Leroy Searle, eds. *Critical Theory since 1965.* Gainesville: University Presses of Florida and Florida State University Press, 1986.

Castronovo, David. "American Literary Criticism 1914 to Present." In *Encyclopedia of American Literature.* Ed. Steven Serafin. New York: Continuum, 1997.

Davis, Robert Con, and Ronald Schleifer, eds. *Contemporary Literary Criticism: Literary and Cultural Studies.* New York and London: Longman, 1989.

Gilmore, Michael T. "The Commodity World of *The Portrait of a Lady.*" *New England Quarterly* 59 (1986), 51–74.

Kirby, David. "The New Candide, or What I Learned in the Theory Wars." *Virginia Quarterly Review* 69 (1993), 393–408.

Lodge, David, ed. *Modern Criticism and Theory: A Reader.* London and New York: Longman, 1988.

———. *Twentieth-Century Literary Criticism: A Reader.* London and New York: Longman, 1972.

Lynn, Steven. *Texts and Contexts: Writing about Literature with Critical Theory.* New York: HarperCollins, 1994.

Macksey, Richard, and Eugenio Donato, eds. *The Languages of Criticism and the Sciences of Man.* Baltimore: Johns Hopkins University Press, 1970.

Righter, William. *The Myth of Theory.* New York: Cambridge University Press, 1994.

Scanlan, Margaret. "Terrorism and the Realistic Novel: Henry James and *The Princess Casamassima.*" *Texas Studies in Literature and Language* 34 (1992), 380–403.

Selden, Raman. *A Reader's Guide to Contemporary Literary Theory.* 2nd ed. Lexington: University Press of Kentucky, 1989.

Winchell, Mark Royden. *Cleanth Brooks and the Rise of Modern Criticism.* Charlottesville: University Press of Virginia, 1996.

MR. POST-EVERYTHING

Deleuze, Gilles, and Leopold von Sacher-Masoch. *Masochism.* 1971. Reprint, New York: Zone Books, 1989.

"THE THING YOU CAN'T EXPLAIN"

Clément, Catherine. *Opera, or The Undoing of Women.* Trans. Betsy Wing. Foreword by Susan McClary. Minneapolis: University of Minnesota Press, 1988.

Freud, Sigmund. *On Dreams.* Vol. 5 of *The Standard Edition of the Complete Psychological Works of Sigmund Freud.* Ed. James Strachey. London: The Hogarth Press and the Institute of Psycho-Analysis, 1958.

Grosz, Elizabeth. *Sexual Subversions: Three French Feminists.* Boston: Allen and Unwin, 1989.

Irons, Glenwood, ed. *Gender, Language, and Myth: Essays on Popular Narrative.* Toronto: University of Toronto Press, 1992.

Kaplan, E. Ann. *Motherhood and Representation: The Mother in Popular Culture and Melodrama.* London and New York: Routledge, 1992.

Leavis, Q. D. *Fiction and the Reading Public.* London: Chatto & Windus, 1932.

McClary, Susan. *Feminine Endings: Music, Gender, and Sexuality.* Minneapolis: University of Minnesota Press, 1991.

Rothenberg, Albert. *The Emerging Goddess: The Creative Process in Art, Science, and Other Fields.* Chicago: University of Chicago Press, 1979.

REVIEWERS IN THE POPULAR PRESS AND THEIR IMPACT ON THE NOVEL

Baym, Nina. *Novels, Readers, and Reviewers: Responses to Fiction in Antebellum America.* Ithaca: Cornell University Press, 1984.

Donoghue, Frank. *The Fame Machine: Book Reviewing and Eighteenth-Century Literary Careers.* Stanford: Stanford University Press, 1996.

Johnson, Robert. "Pop Criticism Provides Non-Academic Readers a Unique Service." *St. Louis Journalism Review* 22 (1993), 16–18.

Klienberger, H. R. *The Novel in England and Germany: A Comparative Study.* London: Oswald Wolff, 1981.

Mott, Frank L. *A History of American Magazines.* 5 vols. Cambridge: Belknap Press of Harvard University Press, 1930–1968.

Smith, Henry Nash. *Democracy and the Novel: Popular Resistance to Classic American Writers*. New York: Oxford University Press, 1978.

Smith, Herbert F. *The Popular American Novel, 1865–1920*. Boston: Twayne Publishers, 1980.

Taylor, John Tinnon. *Early Opposition to the English Novel: The Popular Reaction from 1760 to 1830*. New York: King's Crown Press, 1943.

Tompkins, J. M. S. *The Popular Novel in England, 1770–1800*. Lincoln: University of Nebraska Press, 1961.

Turnell, Martin. *The Rise of the French Novel*. New York: New Directions, 1978.

Women in Publishing. *Reviewing Reviews: A Woman's Place on the Book Page*. London: Journeyman Press, 1987.

M. L. ROSENTHAL AND OUR LIFE IN POETRY

Rosenthal, M. L. *Our Life in Poetry: Selected Essays and Reviews*. New York: Persea Books, 1991.

What Is a Book?

GHOSTS AND GADABOUTS

Fiedler, Leslie. *Love and Death in the American Novel*. New York: Stein and Day, 1966.

Hutchinson, Stuart. *Henry James: An American as Modernist*. London: Vision Press, 1982.

Martin, Jay. *Harvests of Change: American Literature, 1865–1914*. Englewood Cliffs, N.J.: Prentice-Hall, 1967.

Matthiessen, F. O. *American Renaissance: Art and Expression in the Age of Emerson and Whitman*. New York: Oxford University Press, 1941.

Reynolds, David S. *Beneath the American Renaissance: The Subversive Imagination in the Age of Emerson and Melville*. New York: Knopf, 1988.

Shulman, Robert. *Social Criticism and Nineteenth-Century American Fictions*. Columbia: University of Missouri Press, 1987.

Spender, Stephen. *Love-Hate Relations: English and American Sensibilities*. London: Hamish Hamilton, 1974.

Young, Philip. *Three Bags Full: Essays in American Fiction.* New York: Harcourt Brace, 1967.

BORN IN THE MARKETPLACE

Baym, Nina. *Novels, Readers, and Reviewers: Responses to Fiction in Antebellum America.* Ithaca: Cornell University Press, 1984.

Bell, Ian F. A., ed. *Henry James: Fiction as History.* Totowa, N.J.: Vision Press and Barnes and Noble, 1984.

Brown, Gillian. *Domestic Individualism: Imagining Self in Nineteenth-Century America.* Berkeley: University of California Press, 1990.

Elliott, Emory, ed. *The Columbia History of the American Novel.* New York: Columbia University Press, 1991.

Fleischmann, Fritz. *American Novelists Revisited: Essays in Feminist Criticism.* Boston: G. K. Hall, 1982.

Hill, Richard. "Overreaching: Critical Agenda and the Ending of *Adventures of Huckleberry Finn.*" *Texas Studies in Literature and Language* 33 (1991), 492–514.

Machor, James L. "Fiction and Informed Reading in Early Nineteenth-Century America." *Nineteenth-Century Fiction* 47 (1992), 320–49.

———, ed. *Readers in History: Nineteenth-Century American Literature and the Contexts of Response.* Baltimore: Johns Hopkins University Press, 1993.

Reynolds, David S. *Walt Whitman's America: A Cultural Biography.* New York: Knopf, 1995.

Ringe, Donald A. *American Gothic: Imagination and Reason in Nineteenth-Century Fiction.* Lexington: University Press of Kentucky, 1982.

Scanlan, Margaret. "Terrorism and the Realistic Novel: Henry James and *The Princess Casamassima.*" *Texas Studies in Literature and Language* 34 (1992), 380–403.

Seltzer, Mark. *Henry James and the Art of Power.* Ithaca: Cornell University Press, 1984.

Smith, Henry Nash. *Democracy and the Novel: Popular Resistance to Classic American Writers.* New York: Oxford University Press, 1978.

Williams, Susan S. " 'Promoting an Extensive Sale': The Production and

Reception of *The Lamplighter.*" *New England Quarterly* 69 (1996), 179–201.

IT ISN'T ABOUT AMERICA, IT *IS* AMERICA

Budd, Louis. "The Recomposition of *Adventures of Huckleberry Finn.*" *Missouri Review* 10 (1987), 113–27.

Cardwell, Guy. *The Man Who Was Mark Twain: Images and Ideologies.* New Haven: Yale University Press, 1991.

Fiedler, Leslie. *Love and Death in the American Novel.* New York: Stein and Day, 1966.

Index